To all my lovely friends and family along the Amalfi Coast who still keep the traditions of this delectable citrus fruit well and truly alive.

Gennaro's Limoni

Vibrant Italian recipes celebrating the lemon

Gennaro Contaldo

Photography by David Loftus

PAVILION

First published in the United Kingdom in 2021 by
Pavilion
43 Great Ormond Street
London
WC1N 3HZ

ISBN 978-1-911663-18-8

A CIP catalogue record for this book is available from the British Library.
10 9 8 7 6 5 4 3 2 1

Reproduction by Rival Colour Ltd. ,UK
Printed and bound by Toppan Leefung Ltd, China
www.pavilionbooks.com

Photographer: David Loftus
Publisher: Helen Lewis
Project editor: Sophie Allen
Copy editor: Stephanie Evans
Proofreader: Vicki Murrell
Design: Laura Russell and Nikki Ellis
Production manager: Phil Brown

CONTENTS

INTRODUCTION

Lemons are precious to me; a symbol of my beloved homeland, they stir up fond memories of my childhood as well as having a wealth of uses. They cleanse, refresh, preserve and are an absolute essential in the home.

Lemons were and still are a part of daily life for the locals of the Amalfi Coast, and even though I came to England 50 years ago, my addiction to this citrus fruit has never ceased. Obviously, I was not able to find the Amalfi variety in the UK back then, but I would always buy the best I could. And when friends and family came to visit, their suitcases would be full of the sweetest of lemons, the absolute best present to remind me of home.

I can recognize whether a lemon is from Amalfi or not – rub the skin and inhale – all of us from the region can tell. Of course, you don't have to use Amalfi lemons to make the recipes in this book; just buy the best unwaxed variety you can find.

It has been an absolute pleasure writing this book – lemons are part of me, my childhood and my culture. Going to my hometown of Minori to shoot part of this book was a sheer joy: visiting the lemon groves, the growers themselves, and friends and family who shared their favourite lemon recipes with me. It was wonderful seeing my friend Valentino make his famous limoncello; Gabriele at the local pastry shop, who showed me how to make candied lemon peel; the chef at my favourite restaurant, for his signature fish dish; Erminia for her delicious rabbit dish; and many others. I am truly blessed to know you all and thank you for keeping alive the traditions of this indispensable citrus fruit.

I hope you enjoy recreating the recipes in this book and love using lemons just as much as I do, and, who knows, you may get addicted too, and insist on carrying a lemon with you wherever you go!

The Amalfi lemon

I know I'm biased but the Amalfi lemon, locally known as the *Sfusato Amalfitano*, is like no other: a huge, elongated-in-shape, knobbly, thick-skinned citrus fruit, but oh-so wonderfully sweet and aromatic, with a soft pith that can be eaten as well. In fact, no part of the lemon is ever wasted – even the leaves are used.

Lemon growing in this area has been a tradition and a way of life for a thousand years. Lemons were brought to the region from the Middle East in the tenth century, and over time, local farmers managed to cross them with local bitter oranges to produce what we know today as the Amalfi lemon. The rich, fertile volcanic soil and favourable climatic conditions of the valleys made it ideal for this citrus fruit to grow so abundantly.

With Amalfi being an important maritime republic at the time, the lemons became a highly sought-after trade item as well as an excellent source of vitamin C for sailors during long voyages. By the nineteenth century, the Amalfi lemon had gained great economic and social value for the area, and transformation of the landscape was finally complete. The once-unproductive rural land above the coastal villages had, over time, been transformed into terraces of lemon cultivation, using wood from local chestnut trees as supports for the plants, and irrigation systems were put in place. Generations of entire families owned terraces and oversaw the cultivation process from start to finish, for perfect lemons to be sold and exported.

Although the favourable conditions allowed for the growth of wonderful lemons, the location of the terraces, being high up, meant that bringing the lemons down to sea level was an arduous task. Unfortunately, in those days, this job was assigned to the women, who were known as *portatrici di limoni*, or lemon carriers. Thankfully, this is no longer the case, but as a young child, I remember seeing these women dressed in their long skirts, with huge baskets perched on their shoulders, carrying kilos and kilos of lemons all the way down the long, steep and often rickety stone paths. Groups of women would often make the journey together and sing, but not classic melodies, rather stories they would tell each other in a sing-song way.

Cultivation of the Amalfi lemon is still carried out using the same traditional methods that have always been used, with strict rules and regulations in place, and each lemon is still picked by hand. The lemons have been given IGP status, which provides official confirmation that they were grown in the area under strict control.

You could say I was 'weaned' on lemons – we always had lemons at home; they were essential not only in the kitchen but for all sorts of household and medicinal purposes. Studies show that the Amalfi lemon has a higher percentage of vitamin C compared to other lemon varieties and its peel has a greater aromatic potency.

The popularity of the Amalfi lemon is seen all over the area's coastal towns and villages, in the form of cakes, pastries, ice cream and the famous granita, as well as in savoury dishes. I remember as a little boy, I would often help the owner of the local café to zest lemons for his granita so I could be rewarded with a cold glass at the end. Whenever I embarked on fishing trips, I would always bring a lemon so I could squeeze the juice onto some fresh limpets. And on my childhood adventures, if I grazed my leg or arm, lemon juice would act as a disinfectant. In fact, even now, I hardly ever leave the house without a lemon. It's a habit I have never grown out of!

9   Introduction

Lemons in the kitchen

I always start my day with a lemon – well, a sliver of zest, which I add to my espresso first thing in the morning. It gives the strong coffee a lovely subtle, refreshing tang. It's a habit I picked up from home in Italy and have enjoyed ever since – even when I stay in hotels overnight, I will ask for a lemon or, more often than not, I will have brought one with me!

When you think of lemons in the kitchen, desserts naturally spring to mind, and there are indeed many wonderful lemon-enhanced ice creams, puddings, cakes and biscuits, but lemons are also fantastic in savoury dishes. From simply drizzling the juice onto freshly cooked fish, to wrapping the fruit's leaves around cheese and meat, no part of the lemon is ever wasted. The spongy white pith can be used in a salad of lemons, often eaten during summer as a refreshing light meal, and is a simple but culinary delight. Pasta and risotto dishes with lemon are a popular choice on restaurant menus along the Amalfi Coast, and the combination of Parmesan and lemon is a match made in heaven! Once you try a simple lemon risotto, you will be hooked, and I'm sure the temptation to squeeze a little juice over it and a lot of other dishes will become a habit!

Often, just a squeeze of lemon or freshly grated zest over a finished dish is all you need to liven up a meal, and it is my preferred dressing for salads and cooked vegetables. Like most Italians, I enjoy a drizzle of lemon juice over a simple grilled steak and other meat dishes, like a *Milanese* (pork or veal covered in breadcrumbs); it not only gives a kick to the meat, but also brings out the flavour.

Lemon is a great addition to drinks too, from a few drops of juice in a glass of water to the ever-popular alcoholic drink limoncello. Made with lemon rinds, this refreshing after-dinner drink is also added to a variety of cocktails.

Often, as kids, we didn't have access to many sweet treats, so when we wanted something sweet, my mother would thinly slice a lemon and drizzle it with sugar. We would eat the lot – peel, pith and flesh – and lick the sweet juices left on the plate! I call it *Dolce dei Poveretti* (Poor Man's Dessert) and I still enjoy it today; it's sweet, tangy and a healthier dessert option.

Household lemons

Growing up, I don't really remember there being household detergents, but I do recall my mother and sisters using lemons to clean. I especially remember lemon juice was used to rub stains off our copper pots and pans, and it was also used to clean the sink and the wooden kitchen table.

Lemons have antiseptic properties, so the juice makes an ideal natural bleach – of course you would need a lot of lemons if you were to use this method for all your cleaning. However, you could combine the juice with vinegar, which is often used for household chores, and the pleasant citrus aroma will disguise the not-so-pleasant vinegar smell.

These days at home, when I have used lemon halves lying around, I never throw them away; instead I put them in the dishwasher on the top rack and run through a cycle – they give off a lovely, subtle lemon fragrance and help your plates sparkle.

Half a lemon will keep your fridge smelling sweet, and will clean and sterilize your microwave, giving it a pleasant fresh smell.

I rub my wooden chopping boards with lemon after using them. And after handling strong-smelling foods like fish, garlic or onion, I wash my hands with lemon juice.

Medicinal lemons

A lemon a day keeps the doctor away

My mother didn't believe much in modern medicine and made her own herbal potions for various minor ailments. One of her most-loved ingredients was lemons, and she made sure I carried one when going out on my adventures.

At the slightest hint of a sniffle, out came the lemons, and she would make *canarino* – hot water infused with thinly pared lemon rind. For a sore throat, she would make me gargle with water and lemon juice, and a grazed knee would be disinfected with a drop or two of lemon juice – it stung but it did the trick! If we had eaten too much, especially after large festive meals, a glass of lemon water was the perfect remedy to aid digestion and feel less bloated. Even headaches and fever would be relieved with warm lemon water.

My older sisters would apply lemon juice to their hair to give it extra shine, as well as using it on their skin to help with spots, rashes and even sunburn.

Lemons are packed full of vitamin C and an abundance of other vital nutrients necessary for wellbeing, and their natural antibacterial properties help to heal the body both inside and out.

It has become scientifically evident that lemons are good for you on so many levels – they can help relieve the effects of colds and flu, high blood pressure, diabetes, strokes, stress, tiredness, eczema, arthritis and respiratory and digestive problems, and they can even aid weight loss. A glass of lemon water a day helps flush out toxins and boosts the immune system, which could in turn prevent many ailments.

SMALL
PLATES

INSALATA DI FINOCCHIO E MELA CON RAGU CALDO AGLI AGRUMI

Fennel and apple salad with a warm citrus dressing

This simple salad is perfect just after Christmas when sweet clementines are still in season and you are in need of something light and refreshing after all the rich festive food! Delicious as part of an antipasto or a light meal served with some grissini (breadsticks). I like to make this with an apple variety native to southern Italy, called Annurca, but it will be equally delicious with whatever eating apples you normally enjoy.

Serves 4–6
1 fennel bulb, thinly sliced (reserve the green
    fronds for garnish)
1 large apple, quartered, cored and thinly sliced
    (peeled if you wish)
2 tbsp extra virgin olive oil, plus extra for drizzling
segments of 2 clementines, membranes removed
segments of ½ lemon, membranes removed,
    roughly chopped into small pieces
5 tbsp water
handful of shaved Parmesan cheese
sea salt and freshly ground black pepper

Arrange the fennel and apple slices on a plate, sprinkle with salt, drizzle with the olive oil and toss well together.

Place the clementine and lemon pieces with the water in a small pan over a medium heat and cook for about 5 minutes until the fruit has softened and the liquid reduced. Remove from the heat and drain away any excess liquid.

Pour the citrus fruit over the fennel and apple slices, top with Parmesan shavings, drizzle with a little more olive oil, sprinkle with black pepper and garnish with some of the green fennel fronds. Serve immediately.

INSALATA DI CECI

Chickpea salad

Chickpeas and lemon go really well together and this salad, which can be eaten warm or cold, is delicious for any occasion – it's perfect as part of an antipasto, served as part of a buffet at parties or as a light meal. It's also very simple to prepare, although because it's made using dried chickpeas, check the recommended cooking times on the packet, and remember you need to allow them to soak overnight.

Serves 4
250g (9oz) dried chickpeas
¼ tsp bicarbonate of soda
1 rosemary sprig
1 thyme sprig
3 sage leaves
3 bay leaves
1 lemon, halved (one half juiced; the other thinly sliced)
4 tbsp extra virgin olive oil
5 mint leaves, finely chopped
6 anchovy fillets
150g (5½oz) Taggiasca olives, pitted
½ red chilli, finely chopped
sea salt

Place the dried chickpeas in plenty of cold water with the bicarbonate of soda (this helps to soften the chickpeas and speeds up cooking time) and leave to soak overnight.

Tie the herbs together to make a bouquet garni. Drain the chickpeas and put in a pan with the herbs and enough fresh cold water to cover. Bring to the boil, then reduce the heat and, covering the pan with a lid, gently simmer for a couple of hours or until the chickpeas are tender.

When tender, drain the chickpeas, reserving some of the cooking water, and allow them to cool a little.

In a small bowl, combine the lemon juice, olive oil, 4 tablespoons of the cooking water and a little salt.

Transfer the chickpeas to a bowl together with the mint, anchovy fillets, olives, lemon slices and red chilli. Pour over the dressing and mix well together. This can be served immediately or when required. It will last in the fridge for a couple of days but bring to room temperature before serving.

INSALATA DI MARE

Mixed seafood salad

Insalata di mare is very popular and eaten in all the coastal towns and villages of Italy. I love the different varieties of seafood that you get in this dish, it's a feast for the eyes and a pleasure to eat! Try to get the freshest seafood you can for maximum flavour. This serves 4 as a starter or 2 for a light lunch. All you need is some good bread to mop up the delicious juices.

Serves 2–4
pared rind of 1 unwaxed lemon
350g (12oz) octopus
200g (7oz) squid
250g (9oz) mussels, scrubbed clean, beards removed
8 razor clams
200g (7oz) raw king prawns
3 tbsp extra virgin olive oil
2 tbsp lemon juice
handful of flat-leaf parsley leaves, roughly chopped
1 garlic clove, finely sliced
¼ fresh red chilli, finely chopped
sea salt
lemon wedges, to serve

Place a saucepan of water with about 3 lemon rind parings over the heat, bring to the boil, then with the help of tongs, dip the octopus tentacles down into the boiling water for a few seconds. Do this a couple more times in order to curl up the tentacles, then drop the entire octopus into the boiling water and leave to cook for about 45 minutes until tender.

Meanwhile, prepare the rest of the seafood. Place another pan of water with a couple more lemon parings over the heat, bring to the boil and cook the squid for 17–20 minutes until tender.

Put the mussels in a saucepan (no liquid), cover with a lid and cook over a medium heat for about 3–4 minutes until the shells open. Any unopened mussels must be discarded. When cool enough to handle, remove most of the mussels from their shells, leaving a few in their shells for decoration, if desired.

continued on next page...

Put the clams and prawns in a pan with a little water and another couple of lemon parings, cover with a lid and cook over a medium heat for about 2 minutes until the clams have opened up and the prawns have turned pink. Strain the liquid through a fine sieve and set aside. Remove the shells from the prawns and from the clams, which you can chop or leave whole. You can also leave a couple of razor clams in their shells for decoration if desired.

When the octopus and squid are cooked, drain and leave to cool. Chop the octopus into chunks and slice the squid into rings, reserving the tentacles.

Combine the extra virgin olive oil, lemon juice, salt, parsley, garlic, chilli and 2 tablespoons of the clam/prawn liquid.

Place the seafood in a bowl, (except any mussels or clams still in their shells) pour the dressing all over and mix well together. Arrange on a serving plate, top with the unshelled seafood and serve with lemon wedges.

INSALATA DI SGOMBRO AFFUMICATO E AGRUMI CON SALSINA DI CAPPERI

Mackerel and citrus fruit salad with a caper dressing

Slightly oily smoked mackerel combines really well with the fresh flavours of both orange and lemon, finished off with a caper and herb dressing and crunchy fennel. This Sicilian-inspired salad is quick to prepare as a deliciously healthy summer lunch or as part of an antipasto, served with lots of good bread to mop up the dressing.

Serves 2
200g (7oz) smoked mackerel fillet
juice of 1 lemon
segments of 1 lemon, membranes removed
juice of ½ orange
segments of 1 orange, membranes removed
20g (¾oz) capers, very finely chopped
3 ½ tablespoons extra virgin olive oil
4 basil leaves, finely chopped
6 mint leaves, finely chopped
50g (1¾oz) fennel, julienned

Discard the skin from the mackerel fillets and flake into pieces. Arrange on a plate and drizzle with orange and lemon juice. Add the orange and lemon segments.

Combine the capers, olive oil, basil and mint and pour over the salad. Arrange the fennel on top and serve.

FRUTAS

PIZZA AL LIMONE CON SALSICCIA, MOZZARELLA E RUCOLA

Lemon-infused pizza with sausage, mozzarella and rocket

On the Amalfi Coast, where large, sweet lemons are in abundance, pizzas are made with slices of lemon and Provola, a local smoked cheese. As Amalfi lemons are not easily obtainable, I decided to make an alternative lemon pizza with zest in the dough, on the topping and a squeeze on the rocket at the end. The combination of lemon, sausage, onion and rosemary works really well and the final handful of rocket at the end adds to the lovely lemony freshness. Try it for a different pizza!

Makes 2 large pizzas or 4 smaller ones

For the dough
500g (1lb 2oz) strong white bread flour, plus extra for dusting
7g sachet dried yeast
1 tsp sea salt
zest of 2 unwaxed lemons
approx. 325ml (11fl oz) lukewarm water

For the topping
3 tbsp extra virgin olive oil
1 large white onion, finely sliced
250g (9oz) Italian pork sausages, skins
    removed and meat crumbled
a few rosemary needles
2 balls of mozzarella (approx. 250g/9oz)
zest of 1 unwaxed lemon
2 handfuls of rocket
extra virgin olive oil
lemon juice
sea salt and freshly ground black pepper

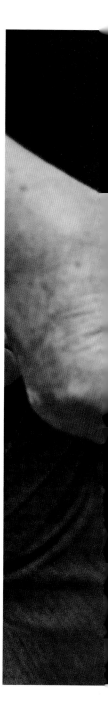

First make the dough. Combine the flour, yeast, salt and lemon zest and gradually stir in enough water to make a dough. Knead the dough for 10 minutes, then cover with a cloth and leave to rest for about 30 minutes.

continued on next page...

Divide the dough into the required number of pieces and knead each one on a lightly floured surface for about 2 minutes. Place on a lightly floured baking tray, cover with a cloth and leave to rest in a warm place for about 1 hour or until doubled in size.

Meanwhile, make the topping. Heat the extra virgin olive oil in a frying pan, add the onion and sweat for a couple of minutes over a medium heat. Stir in the sausage meat, rosemary needles and some salt and pepper and continue to cook for a couple of minutes. Remove from the heat and set aside. Slice the mozzarella into small pieces and also set aside.

Preheat the oven to 220°C fan/200°C/gas mark 6.

Take each piece of dough and flatten to make a pizza base (thickness according to your preference), then top with the sausage mixture, scatter over pieces of mozzarella, grate the lemon zest all over and bake in the oven for about 10 minutes.

Toss the rocket in a little extra virgin olive oil and lemon juice. Remove the pizzas from the oven, top with dressed rocket and serve.

BRUSCHETTA CON SALMONE AFFUMICATO E MASCARPONE AL LIMONE

Bruschetta with smoked salmon and lemon mascarpone

These make a lovely starter or finger food at parties. You can make the bruschetta as large or small as you like. Creamy mascarpone cheese combines really well with lemon and is a perfect combination with smoked salmon.

Makes 4 large bruschette
4 slices smoked salmon (approx. 100g/3½oz)
zest and juice of 1 unwaxed lemon
100g (3½oz) mascarpone
5 tsp finely chopped dill
4 slices sourdough bread
sea salt and freshly ground black pepper

Drizzle the smoked salmon with a little of the lemon juice, sprinkle with a little black pepper and set aside.

Whisk the mascarpone with about 4 tsp of the lemon juice, half the lemon zest, the dill and a little salt until creamy. Taste and adjust the amount of juice and salt accordingly.

Toast the slices of sourdough, place a slice of smoked salmon on each and top with mascarpone, sprinkle with the remaining lemon zest and serve. Or you could spread a little of the mascarpone on the bread and top with salmon.

PURE' DI CECI

Chickpea purée

This simple chickpea purée can be served as an accompaniment to meat or veggie dishes, as a dip or topped on crostini as a starter or snack. It can be served hot or cold, and you can make it in advance and store in the fridge for a couple of days; gently reheat or serve at room temperature.

Serves 4–6
200g (7oz) dried chickpeas
¼ tsp bicarbonate of soda
2 rosemary sprigs, one left whole,
    needles stripped from the other
2 parings of rind and juice of 1 unwaxed lemon
5 anchovy fillets
1 small garlic clove, peeled
1 tbsp extra virgin olive oil
6 tbsp chickpea cooking water
approx. 150ml (5fl oz) water

Place the dried chickpeas in plenty of cold water with the bicarbonate of soda (this helps to soften the chickpeas and speeds up cooking time) and leave to soak overnight.

Drain the chickpeas, then place in a pan with the whole rosemary sprig and lemon rind, cover with fresh water, bring to the boil and simmer for about 2 hours – or check the packet for cooking instructions.

When the chickpeas are tender, drain, reserving some of the cooking water, and discard the rosemary sprig and lemon rind.

Put the cooked chickpeas and the remaining ingredients, except the water, into a blender or mixer and whizz, gradually adding the water, until you obtain a smooth consistency.

PINZIMONIO

Raw vegetables with herb and lemon dip

Pinzimonio is a light classic Italian antipasto dish traditionally of crunchy raw vegetables served with a simple dip of seasoned extra virgin olive oil, to which some add vinegar or lemon juice. To give it a bit of a colourful twist, I have added herbs that have been blanched to soften and of course I use lemon juice to liven it up! You can use whatever raw vegetables you prefer and don't have to use the ones I have suggested – try radishes, spring onions, tender artichokes, Belgian endive, cucumber and whatever else you spot at the market. Perfect to serve as part of an antipasto or at parties with a large plate of different, colourful veggies at the centre of the table. You could also serve additional dips, or the Lemon Mayo and Simple Salad Dressing (see page 182).

Serves 4
2 carrots, peeled and sliced lengthways into batons
2 celery sticks, halved and sliced into batons
1 fennel bulb, sliced lengthways into about 8 pieces
leaves of ½ trevisano (long narrow) radicchio
½ red pepper, deseeded and sliced
½ yellow pepper, deseeded and sliced
2 handfuls of flat-leaf parsley leaves
2 handfuls of basil leaves
4 tbsp extra virgin olive oil
2 tbsp lemon juice
sea salt

Prepare the vegetables and arrange on a platter.

Put the parsley and basil in a small pan with a little water, bring to the boil and blanch for a couple of minutes. Drain and place the herbs in a mixer with extra virgin olive oil, lemon juice and a little salt, whizz until the herbs are chopped and everything is nicely amalgamated. Pour into a small bowl and serve with the prepared vegetables.

LIMONI RIPIENI AL FORNO DI VALENTINO

Valentino's baked filled lemons

This dish was made for me by my good friend Valentino, who uses the best, freshest anchovies, wonderful Amalfi lemons and local mozzarella to create an unusual, delicious antipasto. You may need a little more or less of the filling ingredients, depending on the size of your lemons. Serve 1 or 2 lemon halves per person for a starter. Valentino's tip: while you could use ready-made dried breadcrumbs to top the lemons, they tend to burn more easily and your own mix of fresh bread and thyme quickly fried will enhance the flavour.

Serves 2–4
2 lemons, washed and dried
12–16 fresh anchovies, heads removed, and cleaned
approx. 15g (½oz) country bread, lightly toasted
4 cherry tomatoes, halved or quartered depending on size
60g (2¼oz) mozzarella, cut into small cubes
extra virgin olive oil
1 large slice of bread, crusts removed, and finely chopped
    to resemble breadcrumbs
a few thyme leaves
sea salt and freshly ground black pepper

Preheat the oven to 160°C fan/180°C/gas mark 4.

Halve the lemons and squeeze the juice. Place the fresh anchovies in a small bowl, pour over the lemon juice, add a pinch of salt and leave to marinate for 15 minutes.

Remove any remaining flesh from the squeezed lemon halves with a small sharp knife and trim the bases so they can stand up. Line the bottom of each half with a small piece of the lightly toasted bread (this will absorb moisture from the other ingredients), then layer with a couple of anchovies, some tomato, mozzarella and a drizzle of extra virgin olive oil, then make another layer.

Heat a splash of extra virgin olive oil in a frying pan over a low to medium heat, add the breadcrumbs, thyme and some salt and pepper and stir-fry for about 30 seconds to allow the flavours to infuse. Top the lemons with this breadcrumb mixture. Place the lemons on a baking dish, drizzle with a little olive oil, cover with foil and bake for 15–17 minutes. About 5 minutes before the end of the cooking time, remove the foil and continue to bake until the mozzarella has melted and the breadcrumbs are golden. Remove from the oven and serve.

SARDINE AL CARPIONE
Lemon-marinated sardines with diced vegetables

Al carpione is a traditional way of marinating fish or meat. It was commonly used in times before fridges were invented, especially in the northern lakes region of Italy where freshwater fish was in abundance. Wine vinegar was typically used, but I find lemon juice is just as good and it acts as a preservative in the same way. Cooking *al carpione* continues, but not for preserving reasons, often to make a delicious antipasto, like this dish.

Serve 1–2 sardines per person
6 sardines, headless but left whole
plain flour, for dusting
8 tbsp mild olive oil
1 carrot, finely chopped
1 celery stick, finely chopped
70g (2½oz) fennel, finely chopped
1 small red onion, finely chopped
½ red (or yellow or orange) pepper, finely chopped
¼ red chilli, finely chopped
6 cocktail gherkins, finely chopped
20g (¾oz) capers
1 tbsp chopped flat-leaf parsley
juice of 1 lemon
sea salt

Pat dry the sardines with kitchen paper and dust in a little plain flour. Heat 6 tablespoons of the olive oil in a frying pan and, when hot, add the sardines and fry for about 2–3 minutes on each side, until golden. Remove from the heat and drain on kitchen paper. Arrange on a serving plate.

In another frying pan, heat the remaining oil and add all the finely chopped vegetables, including the gherkins and capers. Stir-fry over a high to medium heat for about 5 minutes until they are slightly soft, but still crunchy. Remove from the heat, season with a little salt to taste, stir in the parsley and lemon juice and, while the veggies are still hot, pour over the sardines, covering completely. Leave to cool at room temperature, then serve.

LIMONI RIPIENI ALLA CREMA DI TONNO

Tuna-filled lemons

Here's something different, which I am sure will impress! This is great served as a refreshing antipasto or as a delicious light lunch with some good bread. I have given you two ways of serving – either in slices or as filled lemon halves. If you are in a hurry, then I would go for the lemon halves as you don't need to wait.

Serves 2–4

2 lemons, washed and dried

For the filling

8 tsp lemon juice (see below)

15g (½oz) capers, finely chopped

4 pitted green olives, finely chopped or leave whole, if desired

130g (4¾oz) drained tinned tuna

100g (3½oz) ricotta

2 anchovy fillets, finely chopped

½ handful of flat-leaf parsley, finely chopped

sea salt and freshly ground black pepper

Trim the top of each lemon until you can see the flesh and, with a small sharp knife, cut around the flesh. Use either a small scoop or teaspoon to remove all the flesh – do this over a bowl to catch all the juice; you want 8 teaspoons of juice for the filling. Set aside.

Combine the filling ingredients and mix until smooth. Fill the lemon cavities with the mixture, packing it in well to avoid any gaps or air bubbles. Wrap the lemons tightly in foil and place in the freezer for an hour.

Remove from the freezer, unwrap the foil and, with a very sharp knife, cut into slices and then arrange on a serving dish. Leave for about 20 minutes at room temperature before serving.

Alternative serving suggestion: slice the lemons in half, scoop out the flesh, make the filling as above and fill each half with the mixture. If serving immediately, there is no need to put in the fridge.

SPIEDINI DI SCAMORZA IN FOGLIE DI LIMONE

Skewers of scamorza cheese wrapped in lemon leaves

This traditional antipasto is served all along the Amalfi Coast; it is really simple, using just two ingredients, but very effective and delicious! The locals use Provola, a cheese that is like a hard smoked mozzarella, but you can more easily find scamorza in Italian delis, which is very similar. The smokiness of the cheese and the subtle flavour of the lemon leaves is a winning combination. You can cook them using a griddle pan, but if you've got a barbeque going, then it's an ideal option. I've made them into skewers, but equally you could simply sandwich the cheese between two lemon leaves and griddle or barbecue them.

Makes 10 little parcels/enough for 2 skewers
200g (7oz) scamorza cheese
10 lemon leaves
1 unwaxed lemon, sliced thinly

Cut the scamorza into 10 slices. Wrap each one in a lemon leaf and thread onto a couple of skewers, alternating with a lemon slice.

Heat a griddle pan. When hot, place the skewers on the griddle to char for a couple of minutes on each side, pressing gently with a fish slice until the cheese begins to melt. Alternatively, place the skewers on a barbecue and turn every couple of minutes as before.

Remove from the heat, slide off the skewers and serve. Simply unwrap the cheese from the lemon leaf and eat together with the charred lemon slices. Enjoy with a simple tomato salad, if desired.

POLPETTINE AL TONNO E LIMONE
Tuna and lemon balls

While I was testing the recipe for Filled Sardines (see page 107) I also made these *polpettine* with the same filling mixture. They are so delicious – once you start to eat one, you can't stop, so perhaps you should increase the quantity! Delicious served as part of an antipasto or as a snack, and kids just love them.

Makes approx. 24 polpettine
120g (4oz) tinned tuna (drained weight)
60g (2¼oz) ricotta
2 tsp finely chopped flat-leaf parsley
2 anchovy fillets, finely chopped, rinsed if salted
10g (¼oz) capers, finely chopped
10g (¼oz) grated Parmesan
zest of 1 unwaxed lemon and 5 tsp lemon juice
plain flour, for dusting
2 eggs, beaten
breadcrumbs, for coating
vegetable or sunflower oil, for frying
sea salt and freshly ground black pepper

Combine the tuna, ricotta, parsley, anchovy fillets, capers, Parmesan, lemon zest and juice to make a smooth but not runny mixture. Check for seasoning and if necessary, add a little salt and black pepper. Make into small balls, roughly the size of chocolate truffles, then dust them in flour, dip into beaten egg and coat in breadcrumbs.

Heat enough oil in a frying pan to come about 1cm (½in) up the sides. When hot, fry the polpettine, in batches if necessary, for about 2 minutes, turning them around until golden all over. Remove and drain on kitchen paper. Serve immediately – but they are equally delicious eaten cold.

INSALATA DI PEPERONI AL LIMONE

Roasted pepper salad

This simple and delicious way of enjoying peppers is often made in Italy during the summer when peppers are in abundance. I have given you the method for roasting them in the oven, but you could place them over a grill or – even better – on a barbecue, which really enhances the flavour. I suggest you make this dish ahead of serving it, because the longer you leave it to marinate, the more delicious it becomes. Serve with good bread, on crostini, as part of an antipasto with cured meats, as a side dish or with Turkey Burgers (see page 131). The addition of lemon to the dressing tastes great and its acidity helps you digest the peppers better.

Serves 2–4
3 peppers – red, yellow, orange
1 garlic clove, finely chopped
a small handful of flat-leaf parsley leaves, roughly chopped
2 tbsp extra virgin olive oil
juice of ½ lemon
sea salt

Preheat the oven to 200°C fan/220°C/gas mark 7.

When the oven is hot, place the whole peppers in a roasting or ovenproof dish and roast until charred and softened, turning from time to time. You will need to allow about 30–40 minutes, depending on the size of the peppers.

Remove from the oven, leave to cool slightly until you can handle them (but don't allow them to get cold as the skin will become too tough to remove) and remove the skin, stalk and seeds. Do this over a bowl to catch the juices and set aside.

Chop the pepper into fillets, arrange on a plate with garlic and parsley and sprinkle with some salt. Combine the extra virgin olive oil, lemon juice and any of the pepper juices and pour over the peppers. Leave to marinate for at least 30 minutes before serving.

INSALATA DI LIMONI D'AMALFI
Amalfi lemon salad

This simple salad is enjoyed along the Amalfi Coast, where delicious sweet lemons grow in abundance. The pith on Amalfi lemons is so thick and spongy that locally this bit is known as '*pane*' (bread). The recipe originated in the area as *cucina povera* (poor people's cooking) because lemons grew everywhere and were cheaply and easily obtainable. I remember eating this refreshing salad when I was growing up and still enjoy it when I return to my home village. To get the authentic flavour of this salad, I recommend you try to get Amalfi lemons as other varieties may taste too sour.

Serves 2–4
1 large Amalfi lemon
sea salt
4 mint leaves, roughly chopped
2 tbsp extra virgin olive oil
1 tbsp red wine vinegar

Carefully remove the rind of the lemon (reserve the parings for another recipe or enjoy in an espresso), but leave the white pith and cut the lemon into slices. Arrange the slices on a plate, sprinkle over some salt and scatter the mint leaves. Combine the extra virgin olive oil and vinegar, pour over and serve.

VEGETABLES

TAGLIATELLE AL LIMONE

Tagliatelle with lemon

Pasta with lemon is very common along the Amalfi Coast and it can be prepared in various ways, often simply with olive oil, lemon and parsley. This is my favourite way, with chilli and garlic. The addition of a little butter at the end makes the sauce lovely and creamy – perfect for the tagliatelle to absorb.

Serves 4
320g (11oz) tagliatelle
3 tbsp extra virgin olive oil
1 garlic clove, finely chopped
¼ red chilli, finely chopped
25g (1oz) butter
zest and juice of 1 unwaxed lemon
20g (¾oz) grated Parmesan cheese,
    plus extra for sprinkling
handful of flat-leaf parsley, finely chopped
sea salt

Bring a large saucepan of salted water to the boil, add the tagliatelle and cook until al dente.

Meanwhile, heat the extra virgin olive oil in a large frying pan, add the garlic and chilli and sweat over a medium heat for a minute or so. Add a ladleful of the pasta water, then the butter and allow to melt, before adding the lemon juice.

Drain the tagliatelle and, using a pair of tongs, add it to the pan and mix well. Stir in the Parmesan and parsley. Serve immediately, sprinkled with the lemon zest and extra Parmesan, if desired.

MEZZELUNE AL LIMONE
Lemon and ricotta-filled pasta

Filled pasta with local ricotta and lemon is a popular dish on restaurant menus along the Amalfi Coast. *Mezzelune* simply means half-moon and these filled pasta parcels served in a creamy buttery and lemon sauce are hard to resist. You need a pasta machine to make these because the dough needs to be really thin.

Serves 4–6 (makes approx. 65 mezzelune)

For the pasta dough
200g (7oz) '00' pasta flour
2 large organic free-range eggs

For the filling
250g (9oz) ricotta
zest of 2 unwaxed lemons, plus extra for sprinkling,
    and 4 tsp lemon juice
15g (½oz) grated Parmesan cheese
sea salt and freshly ground black pepper

For the sauce
100g (3½oz) butter
20 mint leaves (optional)
4 tsp lemon juice
40g (1¼oz) grated Parmesan cheese,
    plus extra for sprinkling

First make the pasta dough. Put the flour into a large bowl or on a clean work surface, make a well in the centre and break in the eggs. With a fork, gradually mix the flour and eggs, then knead with your hands until you obtain a smooth dough. Shape into a ball, wrap in clingfilm and leave to rest in the fridge for about 30 minutes.

Meanwhile, prepare the filling. Drain the ricotta of any liquid, then place in a bowl and combine with lemon zest, lemon juice, grated Parmesan and some salt and pepper.

Remove the dough from the fridge and divide into quarters, using one piece at a time. Rewrap the pieces you are not using in the clingfilm to prevent the pasta from drying out.

continued on next page...

Roll the piece of pasta through a pasta machine, working through the settings until the pasta is paper-thin. Place the sheet of pasta on a lightly floured work surface and cut out circles with a 6-cm (2½-inch) round cutter and lightly brush the edges with a little water. Place a little filling in the centre, fold over into a half moon shape, pressing down with your fingers, then make small indentations with a fork around the sealed edge. Gather up all the pasta trimmings, re-roll and repeat. Continue with the remaining dough pieces and filling.

When you have made all the mezzelune, place a large saucepan of salted water over the heat, bring to the boil and drop in the mezzelune a few at a time to cook for about 3½ minutes.

Meanwhile, make the sauce. Put the butter in a large frying pan with the mint leaves (if using) and allow to melt over a medium to high heat, then add the lemon juice.

Once the mezzelune are cooked, use a slotted spoon or spider to lift them out of the water and place in the frying pan with a couple of tablespoons of the cooking water. Cook over a medium to high heat for a minute or so, shaking the pan. Add the Parmesan and gently mix. Remove from the heat and serve immediately with an extra sprinkling of Parmesan and lemon zest.

LASAGNE CON ZUCCHINE E BESCIAMELLA DI LIMONE

Courgette lasagne with lemon bechamel sauce

Simple to prepare, this light, vegetarian lasagne with a refreshing hint of lemon makes a perfect meal at any time. Delicious served with a mixed side salad.

Serves 4

approx. 350g (12oz) courgettes, thinly sliced lengthways
a little extra virgin olive oil, for brushing
8–10 lasagne sheets (use easy-cook lasagne that
   doesn't need presoaking)
a few basil leaves
1 ball of mozzarella cheese, roughly chopped
30g (1oz) grated Parmesan cheese
1 x quantity Lemon Bechamel Sauce (see page 184)
grated lemon zest, to serve

Place a griddle pan over the heat. Lightly brush the courgette slices with some extra virgin olive oil. When the pan is hot, cook the courgette slices for a couple of minutes on each side until golden brown. Remove and set aside.

Preheat the oven to 180°C fan/200°C/gas mark 6.

Meanwhile, make the bechamel sauce.

Spread a little of the sauce over the base of a 23 x 18cm (9 x 7in) ovenproof dish, then add a single layer of lasagne sheets. Place some courgette slices on top, scatter a few basil leaves, then add a layer of lemon sauce and sprinkle with some mozzarella pieces and Parmesan. Continue with these layers until you have used all the ingredients, finishing with sauce, mozzarella and Parmesan. Cover the dish with foil and bake for 15 minutes. Remove the foil and continue to bake for a further 15 minutes until golden brown and bubbling.

Remove from the oven, leave to rest for 5 minutes, then serve with a little freshly grated lemon zest.

PASTA E CECI AL FINOCCHIETTO E LIMONE

Pasta and chickpeas with fennel and lemon

Pasta and chickpeas is a popular dish all over Italy – certainly one that reminds me of my childhood – especially during the winter when we used a lot of dried beans and pulses to make hearty meals like this one. The tang of lemon combines so well with earthy chickpeas and I often find myself squeezing extra juice over my portion. Wild fennel (herb fennel) is much used in Italian cooking but if you can't find any, or you find the taste too strong, simply omit it.

Serves 4
200g (7oz) dried chickpeas
¼ tsp bicarbonate of soda
3 tbsp extra virgin olive oil
2 small carrots, finely chopped
2 garlic cloves, left whole and squashed
100g (3½oz) fennel bulb, finely chopped
20g (¾oz) wild fennel fronds, roughly chopped (optional)
thinly pared rind of 1 unwaxed lemon
1.8 litres (generous 3 pints) water
200g (7oz) tagliatelle, broken into little pieces
sea salt and freshly ground black pepper
To serve
Parmesan cheese, grated
1 unwaxed lemon, zested then quartered

Place the dried chickpeas in plenty of cold water with the bicarbonate of soda (this helps to soften the chickpeas and speeds up cooking time) and leave to soak overnight.

The next day, heat the extra virgin olive oil in a large saucepan, add the carrots, garlic and fennel bulb and sweat over a medium heat for 2–3 minutes. Drain the chickpeas and stir into the pan with wild fennel (if using) and lemon rind. Add the water, bring to the boil and simmer over a medium heat for about 2 hours (check the instructions on the packet) until the chickpeas are cooked.

When the chickpeas are cooked, add some salt and pepper to taste, increase the heat, add the pasta – you may need a little more boiling water – and cook until the pasta is al dente.

Remove from the heat and serve with grated Parmesan, freshly grated lemon zest and the lemon quarters for squeezing.

FARFALLE CON CAPPERI E LIMONE

Farfalle with capers and lemon

Here's a very quick and easy summery pasta dish, one that's made with very few ingredients, but is extremely tasty. Make sure you use good-quality capers in salt and carefully peel the lemon so you don't include the white pith. Serve with a simple tomato salad for a perfect no-fuss al fresco lunch or dinner. It is of course delicious served at any time of the year – especially when you are in a hurry.

Serves 4
400g (14oz) farfalle
30g (1oz) capers in salt, rinsed and drained
pared rind of 1 unwaxed lemon and 4 tsp juice
handful of flat-leaf parsley leaves
4 tbsp extra virgin olive oil
sea salt and freshly ground black pepper

Bring a large pan of salted water to the boil and cook the farfalle until al dente.

Meanwhile, very finely chop the capers, lemon peel and parsley and combine with the extra virgin olive oil and lemon juice.

Drain the pasta, place in a large bowl, pour over the sauce, mix well and serve immediately with a little freshly ground black pepper.

LINGUINE CON PESTO DI MELANZANE AL PROFUMO DI LIMONE

Linguine with lemon-infused aubergine pesto

The combination of aubergines and lemon works really well together in this delicious pasta dish. The sauce is made a little like a pesto, but I have only blended the aubergine, adding the rest of the ingredients afterwards so that the flaked almonds give a bit of a crunch to the dish.

Serves 4
500g (1lb 2oz) aubergines
15g (½oz) grated Parmesan cheese, plus extra to serve
zest of 1 unwaxed lemon and 2 tsp lemon juice
30g (1oz) flaked almonds, toasted and roughly chopped
350g (12oz) linguine
10 mint leaves, finely chopped
sea salt and freshly ground black pepper

Preheat the oven to 200°C fan/220°C/gas mark 7. Wash the aubergines, dry well and prick all over with a fork. Place in the hot oven and bake for 30–40 minutes until soft. Remove from the oven and allow to cool. When cool enough to handle, cut the aubergines in half lengthways, scoop out the flesh and discard the skins. Place in a sieve over a bowl and press with the back of a spoon to remove the excess water. Transfer to a mixer or blender and whizz until you obtain a smooth consistency.

Scrape the purée into a large bowl and combine with the Parmesan, half the lemon zest, the lemon juice, almonds and some salt and pepper.

Bring a large saucepan of salted water to the boil, add the linguine and cook until al dente. Drain, reserving some of the cooking water.

Add a little of the pasta cooking water to the aubergine mixture, then with the aid of a pair of tongs, add the linguine and mint leaves. Mix well together and serve immediately with a sprinkling of Parmesan and the remaining lemon zest.

GNOCCHI AL LIMONE

Lemon gnocchi

Freshly made potato gnocchi are always a favourite in our household. The addition of a little lemon zest adds freshness and it marries well with the butter, mint and lemon sauce. When we tested this recipe, I served it to the family for lunch; the gnocchi disappeared in seconds and I have never seen such clean plates!

Serves 4–6
1kg (2lb 4oz) potatoes
300g (10½oz) plain flour
1 large egg, beaten
zest and juice of 1 unwaxed lemon (juice reserved for the sauce)
rice flour, for dusting
sea salt

For the sauce
100g (3½oz) butter
8 mint leaves, left whole
4 tsp lemon juice
30g (1oz) grated Parmesan cheese,
    plus extra to serve

To make the gnocchi, boil the potatoes in their skins until cooked, drain, allow to cool slightly, then remove the skins and mash. Combine with the flour, egg, a little salt to taste and half the lemon zest, then mix until you obtain a soft dough. Sprinkle a little rice flour over a work surface and roll out the dough into long sausage shapes. Using a sharp knife, cut into roughly 2cm (¾in) lengths. Set aside.

Bring a large saucepan of lightly salted water to the boil. Drop the gnocchi into the water, in batches, and simmer for a minute or so until they rise to the top. Meanwhile, put the butter in a large frying pan, allow to melt with the mint leaves and lemon juice.

Remove the gnocchi with a slotted spoon, and add to the butter sauce with a little of the cooking water, cook for a minute or so until all the gnocchi are coated in the sauce, add the Parmesan, mix well together and serve immediately with extra Parmesan and the remaining lemon zest.

RISOTTO AL FINOCCHIO E LIMONE
Fennel and lemon risotto

Fennel and lemon go really well together (see the pasta and chickpea recipe on page 58) and combine perfectly in a risotto. I have added the juice of a whole lemon into this recipe, giving it a lovely lemony flavour, but you could use less if you prefer. You could also add a knob of butter at the end, but I prefer to leave this risotto deliciously light.

Serves 2
approx. 725ml (generous 1¼ pints) hot vegetable stock
4 tsp extra virgin olive oil
1 banana shallot, finely chopped
100g (3½oz) fennel, finely sliced – include fronds
    if you like or use to garnish
140g (5oz) risotto rice (carnaroli, vialone nano or arborio)
zest and juice of 1 unwaxed lemon
a small handful of flat-leaf parsley, roughly chopped
20g (¾oz) grated Parmesan cheese, plus extra
    for sprinkling if desired
freshly ground black pepper

Place the vegetable stock in a saucepan over a low heat to keep it warm.

In another pan, heat the extra virgin olive oil, add the shallot and fennel and sweat over a medium heat for a couple of minutes. Add the rice and stir with a wooden spoon to coat all the grains in the oil. Add some or all of the lemon juice and cook, stirring continuously, until the liquid is nearly all absorbed. Add a couple of ladlefuls of hot stock, stirring until absorbed and continue adding and stirring for about 15 minutes until the rice is cooked – it should be soft on the outside but al dente in the centre. (You may not need all of the stock, or you may need a little more.)

Remove from the heat and stir in the parsley and Parmesan. Serve immediately, scattered with lemon zest, black pepper and extra Parmesan if desired.

CARCIOFI AL LIMONE

Braised lemon artichokes

This simple artichoke dish can be enjoyed as a side to most meat dishes or as a main course served with some good bread. Please don't be put off by the preparation of artichokes; once you've done one, you will know they are easy to prepare. The addition of lemon juice gives the artichokes a lovely tangy fresh flavour.

Serves 4 as a side or 2 as a main
juice of 2 lemons, plus a little extra
   for the acidulated water
4 medium-sized globe artichokes
4 tbsp extra virgin olive oil
1 onion, finely sliced
1 tablespoon capers
handful of flat-leaf parsley, roughly chopped
125ml (4fl oz) water
sea salt and freshly ground black pepper

For the acidulated water, fill a medium-sized bowl with water, add a few drops of lemon juice and set aside. This prevents the artichokes from turning black as you prepare them.

To prepare the artichokes, rinse under cold running water, slice off the top quarter and most of the stem with a sharp knife. Use scissors to snip off the sharp thorns. Cut the artichokes into quarters and carefully remove the hairy choke and place them in the acidulated water until you are ready to use.

Drain the artichokes well, pat dry with a tea towel and season well with salt and pepper. Heat the extra virgin olive oil in a large frying pan, add the artichokes and stir-fry over a high heat for 2–3 minutes until golden on all sides. Remove the artichokes and set aside. Add the onion to the same pan and sweat over a medium heat for 3 minutes. Return the artichokes to the pan with the capers and parsley. Add the lemon juice and water, bring to the boil, reduce the heat and simmer with a lid on for about 10 minutes until the artichokes are tender and cooked through. Remove from the heat and serve.

VELLUTATA DI ZUCCA AL PROFUMO DI LIMONE

Pumpkin soup with lemon

Pumpkin and lemon is a winning combination, which I had never tried until my nephew in Italy told me how good it is. Now I always add a squeeze of lemon to this dish!

Serves 4
2 tbsp extra virgin olive oil
1 red onion, finely chopped
½ red chilli, finely chopped (optional)
500g (1lb 2oz) pumpkin (prepared weight),
    chopped into small chunks
1 potato (approx. 150g/5½oz), peeled
    and chopped into small chunks
1 rosemary sprig, needles stripped and roughly chopped
700ml (1¼ pints) hot vegetable stock
zest and juice of ½ unwaxed lemon

Heat the extra virgin olive oil in a medium-sized saucepan, add the onion and chilli (if using) and sweat for a couple of minutes. Stir in the pumpkin, potato and rosemary and sweat for a further 2–3 minutes. Add the hot stock, bring to the boil, then reduce the heat and simmer for about 25–30 minutes until the pumpkin is soft. Blitz to a creamy consistency, stir in the lemon juice, check for seasoning and serve with a sprinkle of the zest.

GRANO SPEZZATO AL PROFUMO DI LIMONE CON VERDURE

Lemon-infused bulgur wheat with vegetables

Bulgur wheat is cracked whole wheat grains and, like couscous, it absorbs the flavour of lemon juice beautifully. The addition of vegetables makes this a simple and healthy main course or you can serve it as an accompaniment to meat dishes.

Serves 2–4
200g (7oz) bulgur wheat
2 parings of rind, zest of ½ unwaxed lemon and
    60ml (2¼fl oz) lemon juice
800ml (28fl oz) vegetable stock
3 tbsp extra virgin olive oil
2 garlic cloves, finely chopped
180g (6oz) courgette, finely cubed
260g (9½oz) aubergine, finely cubed
6 baby plum tomatoes, quartered
6 mint leaves, finely chopped
sea salt

Place the bulgur wheat, lemon rind and vegetable stock in a saucepan, bring to the boil and simmer for about 10 minutes until the liquid is absorbed and the bulgur is cooked – check the packet instructions for timings.

Meanwhile, heat the extra virgin olive oil in a frying pan, add the garlic and sweat for a minute. Add the courgette, aubergine and some salt and stir-fry over a medium heat for about 10 minutes until tender but not mushy. About halfway through, stir in the tomatoes.

When the bulgur wheat is cooked, remove from the heat, discard the rind and stir in the lemon juice and mint. Stir in half the vegetables, place on a serving dish, top with the remaining vegetables and serve with freshly grated lemon zest.

FAGIOLINI CON LIMONE E BRICIOLE

Sautéed green beans with breadcrumbs and lemon

These beans make a delicious accompaniment to meat and fish dishes or the Frittata (see page 79). The breadcrumbs add bulk to the beans, so the recipe can also be enjoyed as a meal in itself, if you prefer.

2–4 servings
200g (7oz) green beans, topped and tailed
2 tbsp extra virgin olive oil
1 banana shallot, finely sliced
juice of ½ lemon
4 mint leaves, roughly torn (optional)
20g (½oz) breadcrumbs
sea salt and freshly ground black pepper

Cook the green beans in slightly salted water for about 7 minutes until tender. Drain, plunge into cold water – this will help retain the green colour – and set aside.

Meanwhile, heat the extra virgin olive oil in a frying pan, add the shallot and sweat for a couple of minutes until softened. Drain the green beans, add to the frying pan and stir-fry for a couple of minutes over a high heat, and season with salt and pepper. Stir in the lemon juice, mint (if using) and breadcrumbs. Reduce the heat and mix well, cooking for just under a minute or so. Remove from the heat and serve.

FAGIOLI CANNELLINI CON VERDURE AL PROFUMO DI LIMONE

Lemon-infused cannellini beans with veggies

I love cooking beans and pulses especially during the winter – I enjoy the ritual of pre-soaking the beans the night before in anticipation of cooking them the next day. Combined with some veggies, this makes a delicious main course and the addition of lemon juice gives it a nice refreshing kick. I normally use cannellini beans, but you can use whichever white beans you prefer. Always check the packet instructions for cooking times.

Serves 4
300g (10½oz) dried cannellini or other white beans
2 tbsp extra virgin olive oil, plus extra for drizzling
1 carrot, finely chopped
½ red onion, finely chopped
1 celery stick, finely chopped
1 small courgette, finely chopped
1 garlic clove, finely chopped
2 rosemary sprigs
800ml (scant 1½ pints) vegetable stock
a paring of unwaxed lemon rind and juice of 1 lemon
freshly ground black pepper

Soak the dried beans in plenty of water and leave overnight. The next day, drain the beans, place in a saucepan, cover with cold water, bring to the boil and cook for about 30 minutes.

Meanwhile, heat the extra virgin olive oil in another large saucepan, add the carrot, onion, celery, courgette, garlic and rosemary and sweat over a medium heat for about 5 minutes. Drain the beans add to the veggies with the stock and lemon peel, bring to the boil, then reduce the heat and continue to cook for about 25 minutes until the beans are cooked. About 5 minutes before the end of cooking time, stir in the lemon juice.

Remove from the heat and serve immediately with a drizzle of extra virgin olive oil and a grinding of black pepper.

FRITTATA AL LIMONE

Lemon frittata

The delicate hint of lemon in this frittata comes first from marinating the onions in lemon juice and adding zest to the actual dish. Serve with a mixed salad and good bread for a tasty vegetarian main course.

Serves 4
400g (14oz) red onions, finely sliced
zest and juice of 1 unwaxed lemon
20g (1oz) butter
3 tbsp extra virgin olive oil
250ml (9fl oz) vegetable stock
6 eggs
handful of flat-leaf parsley, finely chopped
40g (1½oz) grated Parmesan cheese
sea salt and freshly ground black pepper

Place the onions in a bowl with the lemon juice and enough cold water to cover the onions. Set aside and leave for 30–60 minutes, then drain well.

Heat the butter and 2 tablespoons of the extra virgin olive oil in a large non-stick frying pan, add the onions and cook over a low heat for 10 minutes, gently stirring. Pour in the stock and continue to cook gently for another 5–6 minutes until the liquid has been absorbed. Remove from the heat and cool slightly.

Meanwhile, beat the eggs then add the parsley, Parmesan, lemon zest, salt and pepper. Stir in the onions.

Return the frying pan to the heat with 1 tablespoon of extra virgin olive oil, add the egg mixture and cook gently for 5–7 minutes until the base is set. Carefully place a large plate over the pan and quickly invert the pan so that the frittata falls onto the plate, then slide it back into the pan to cook the other side. Alternatively, if you don't want to flip the frittata, place the frying pan under a hot grill until the frittata is golden brown. (You may need to protect the handle of your pan.) Serve hot or cold.

RISOTTO AL LIMONE

Lemon risotto

Tangy and creamy, this lovely risotto is quick and simple to prepare. When my kitchen cupboards are bare, this is my quick go-to meal. The rice absorbs the lemon juice and its flavour really comes through. I love the strong lemony taste, but if you prefer, use a little less lemon juice.

Serves 4
2 tablespoons extra virgin olive oil
40g (1½oz) butter
1 small onion, finely chopped
½ celery stick, finely chopped
300g (10½oz) risotto rice (carnaroli, vialone nano or arborio)
zest and juice of 2 unwaxed lemons
approx. 1.5 litres (1¾ pints) hot vegetable stock
35g (1¼oz) grated Parmesan cheese,
    plus extra for sprinkling
sea salt and freshly ground black pepper
a small handful of basil leaves, roughly torn, to serve

Heat the extra virgin olive oil and half the butter in a pan, add onion and celery and sweat over a medium heat for a couple of minutes until softened. Add the rice and stir with a wooden spoon until each grain is coated in the oil and butter. Stir in the lemon juice and cook, stirring continuously, until the liquid is nearly all absorbed. Add a couple of ladlefuls of hot stock, stirring until absorbed. Continue to do this for about 15–17 minutes until the rice is cooked – it should be soft on the outside but al dente in the centre.

Remove from the heat, beat in the remaining butter, grated Parmesan, a little salt and pepper to taste, and lemon zest. Serve with freshly torn basil leaves and an extra sprinkling of grated Parmesan.

BROCCOLI ALL'AGLIO, PEPERONCINO E LIMONE

Broccoli with garlic, chilli and lemon

This is how I've always enjoyed lightly boiled vegetables – with some good extra virgin olive oil, garlic, chilli and lemon. This simple combination livens up the veg and makes a perfect side dish to meat and fish. I enjoy a plate of this on its own with lots of good bread.

Serves 4
750g (1lb 10oz) longstem broccoli
  or broccoli florets
2 tbsp extra virgin olive oil
1 garlic clove, very finely chopped
½ red chilli, finely chopped
zest and juice of ½ unwaxed lemon
sea salt

Place a pan of water over the heat, bring to the boil and cook the broccoli for about 3 minutes until tender.

Meanwile, heat the extra virgin olive oil in a frying pan, add the garlic and chilli and sweat for a minute. Using a slotted spoon or spider, drain the broccoli and add to the frying pan, stir-fry over a medium heat for a couple of minutes, adding the lemon juice and zest and a little salt to taste. Serve immediately.

ASPARAGI CON UOVA IN CAMICIA CON SALSINA AL BURRO E LIMONE

Asparagus with a creamy butter and lemon sauce with poached eggs

Butter, lemon and Parmesan combine so well with this classic northern Italian dish of asparagus and eggs. Typically it is made without lemon, but the addition of both juice and zest really give this dish a pleasant kick. Serve with lots of good bread to mop up the delicious creamy juices. Ideal served as a brunch or light lunch.

Serves 2–4
500g (1lb 2oz) asparagus
4 organic free-range eggs
100g (3½oz) butter
zest of 1 unwaxed lemon and 50ml (2fl oz) juice,
    plus a little extra zest for sprinkling
30g (1oz) grated Parmesan cheese,
    plus a little extra for sprinkling
freshly ground black pepper

Snap off the hard stems of the asparagus and wash the stalks under cold running water. Place in a pan with some water, bring to the boil and cook for about 2–3 minutes, depending on the thickness of your asparagus, until just tender.

At the same time, put a second pan of water over the heat and, when it boils, carefully crack the eggs into the water (or into a cup first) and poach for 3–4 minutes until the whites are set but the yolks are still nice and runny.

When the asparagus are ready, drain and place them on a clean tea towel to dry, then arrange on plates. Melt the butter in a small pan, add the lemon zest and juice, turn up the heat, stir in the Parmesan and the sauce will begin to thicken slightly, then pour over the asparagus.

Lift out the poached eggs with a slotted spoon, dry on a tea towel and place on top of the asparagus. Sprinkle with a little Parmesan, lemon zest and freshly ground black pepper. Serve immediately with lots of good bread to mop up the sauce.

SCAPECE DI ZUCCHINI AL LIMONE

Lemon-marinated courgettes

This traditional Neapolitan dish was originally made as a way of preserving courgettes when they were in season, but wine vinegar was always used. The dish is still made with vinegar today and usually served with a selection of antipasti. Lemon juice preserves just as well and is ideal for anyone who dislikes the strong taste of vinegar. Perfect served as part of an antipasto or as an accompaniment to fish, such as the Baked Rolled Sole Fillets on page 104.

Serves 4
vegetable oil, for frying
360g (12½oz) courgettes, washed,
    dried and thinly sliced into rounds
1 garlic clove, very finely chopped
10 mint leaves, finely chopped
zest of 1 unwaxed lemon and 4 tsp juice
sea salt
a little lemon zest, to serve

Pour vegetable oil into a frying pan to a depth of about 1cm (½in) and place over the heat. When it is hot, drop in the courgette slices and fry for about 3–4 minutes until golden. Drain on kitchen paper, then place in a bowl with a sprinkling of salt, garlic, mint leaves and lemon juice. Toss together and leave to rest for at least 20 minutes. Sprinkle with some freshly grated lemon zest before serving.

FIORI DI ZUCCHINE RIPIENI
Filled courgette flowers

This has got to be one of the nicest ways of enjoying vegetables, not only pretty to look at but delicious and, once you start eating them, you will wish you had made more! When I first came to England, I was so surprised that people would get rid of the flowers – they are so popular in Italy and we use them in all sorts of recipes. Courgette flowers are available during spring and summer so look out for them at the market or greengrocer or perhaps you grow your own. You may find you need more or less courgette flowers depending on their size.

Serves 4
8 courgette flowers
abundant vegetable oil, for deep-frying
lemon zest, to serve

For the filling
250g (9oz) ricotta
35g (1¼oz) grated Parmesan
juice of 1 small lemon
30g (1oz) breadcrumbs
½ handful of basil leaves, finely chopped
sea salt and freshly ground black pepper

For the batter
3 eggs, separated
pinch of sea salt
2 tsp lemon juice
3 tbsp plain flour

First make the filling by combining all the ingredients. Place the mixture into a piping bag if you have one and set aside.

Carefully open up the courgette flowers from the tip, remove any stamens and fill each one with the ricotta mixture. Close the flower by gently twisting the end of the petals to seal.

Beat the egg yolks until nice and creamy. In another clean bowl, whisk the egg whites with 2 teaspoons of lemon juice and a pinch of salt until stiff, then gently fold into the egg yolks and fold in the plain flour.

continued on next page...

In the meantime, heat plenty of oil in a large pan to deep fry the flowers. Take the filled flowers one by one, holding by the stem, and dip into the egg mixture, gently coating the whole flower. Place in the hot oil and fry for about 3 or 4 minutes until golden-brown. Turn during frying so they have an even golden colour.

Remove, drain on kitchen paper and serve immediately with a sprinkling of freshly grated lemon zest. Delicious enjoyed with a drizzle of lemon juice.

FISH

SPAGHETTI CON ACCIUGHE E NOCI AL PROFUMO DI LIMONE

Spaghetti with anchovies, walnuts and lemon juice

It's quite common to serve pasta with anchovies and walnuts, especially in southern Italy, when the fridge is bare and you need to prepare something quick and easy. I have elaborated on it here with the addition of capers, parsley and tomatoes – that's what I had in my store cupboard when testing this recipe! The addition of lemon juice really gives a tangy zing to the dish and I love to add more when eating.

Serves 2
200g (7oz) spaghetti
3 tablespoons extra virgin olive oil
1 garlic clove, finely sliced
15 capers
12 anchovy fillets, rinsed if salted
5 sweet baby plum tomatoes, halved
10g (¼oz) grated Parmesan cheese, plus extra to serve
juice of ½ lemon, plus extra to serve
handful of flat-leaf parsley, roughly chopped
knob of butter
30g (1oz) walnuts, roughly chopped
sea salt and freshly ground black pepper

Bring a large saucepan of salted water to the boil, add the spaghetti and cook until al dente.

Meanwhile, heat the extra virgin olive oil in a frying pan, add the garlic and capers and sweat for a minute or so over a medium heat. Add the anchovy fillets and, mixing with a wooden spoon, cook until dissolved. Stir in the tomatoes and about 6 tablespoons of the hot pasta cooking water and cook over a medium heat for 5 minutes.

Drain the pasta and, using a pair of tongs, add it to the pan, mixing everything together over the heat. Stir in the Parmesan, lemon juice, parsley, butter and a grinding of black pepper, and mix well together. Serve immediately, sprinkled with the chopped walnuts, some extra Parmesan and a squeeze of lemon.

L'INSALATA DI MERLUZZO DI MAMMA

My mum's cod salad

This was my mum's recipe, which she would often cook for my sister and me. The addition of the cooking water was to make the dish go further by dipping bread into the sauce and mopping up all the juices. It was, and still is, one of my favourite ways of enjoying fish – it's simple, delicious and reminds me of my mamma. For Christmas Eve, we would have a similar salad made with *baccala* (salted cod), which is traditionally eaten during the festive season. This dish makes a lovely sharing platter as an antipasto or can be enjoyed as a light main course with lots of good bread.

Serves 4–6
550g (1lb 4oz) cod fillet
4 tbsp extra virgin olive oil
2 tbsp lemon juice
1 garlic clove, finely sliced
a small handful of flat-leaf parsley leaves, finely chopped
8 green stoned olives, halved or sliced
a little red chilli, finely chopped (optional)
sea salt

Poach the fish in slightly salted water for about 5 minutes or so until cooked through. Drain, but reserve some of the cooking water. Place the cooked cod on a serving dish or divide between individual plates.

Combine the extra virgin olive oil, lemon juice, garlic, some salt, parsley and 3 tablespoons of the cooking water, whisk well together and pour over the fish. Top with green olives and sprinkle with a little red chilli, if desired. Serve with lots of good bread to mop up the dressing.

LINGUINE CON PESTO AL PISTACCHIO E TONNO

Linguine with pistachio pesto and tuna

This simple pasta dish is a complete meal. The tangy lemon flavour gives a lovely kick to tinned tuna. It's worth making more pesto than the amount you need for this recipe; covered, it keeps for about three days in the fridge and you can serve it with pasta on another occasion or use it to top crostini.

Serves 4
320g (11½oz) linguine
4 tbsp extra virgin olive oil
2 garlic cloves, finely chopped
3–4 tins tuna, drained (drained weight approx. 320g/11½oz)
zest of 1 unwaxed lemon and a squeeze of juice
sea salt and freshly ground black pepper

For the pesto
200g (7oz) pistachio nuts (unsalted)
35g (1¼oz) Parmesan cheese, grated
zest of 1 unwaxed lemon
5 basil leaves
½ garlic clove
160ml (5½fl oz) extra virgin olive oil
140ml (4½fl oz) warm water

First make the pesto. Put all the ingredients into a blender and whizz to a smooth consistency. Set aside.

Place a large pan of salted water over the heat, bring to the boil and cook the linguine until al dente.

Meanwhile, heat the extra virgin olive oil in a large frying pan, add the garlic and sweat over a medium heat for a minute. Add the tuna chunks, a little salt and pepper to taste and cook for a minute or so to allow the flavours to infuse. Drain the linguine and mix with the pesto and the tuna and stir well together. Sprinkle with lemon zest, a squeeze of lemon and serve immediately.

RISOTTO AI GAMBERI E LIMONE
Prawn and lemon risotto

Lovely creamy lemony risotto with the addition of king prawns is a match made in heaven! Delicate, light and a perfect meal at any time. Try to get the freshest prawns you can for maximum flavour.

Serves 2
2 tbsp extra virgin olive oil
1 banana shallot, finely chopped
8 raw king prawns, shelled and roughly chopped
140g (5oz) risotto rice (carnaroli,
    vialone nano or arborio)
3 tbsp lemon juice, plus extra for drizzling
700ml (1¼ pints) hot vegetable stock
    (you may need a little extra)
20g (¾oz) butter
zest of ½ unwaxed lemon
a small handful of flat-leaf parsley leaves, finely chopped

Heat the extra virgin olive oil in a pan, add the shallot and prawns and sweat over a medium heat for a couple of minutes until the shallot has softened and the prawns have coloured slightly. Add the rice and stir with a wooden spoon until each grain is coated in the oil. Stir in the lemon juice and cook, stirring continuously, until the liquid is almost all absorbed. Add a ladleful of hot stock, stirring until absorbed and continue adding and stirring for about 15–17 minutes, until the rice is cooked – it should be soft on the outside but al dente on the inside.

Remove from the heat, beat in the butter, stir in the lemon zest and parsley, check for seasoning and serve immediately with a drizzle of lemon juice, if desired.

BRANZINO ALL'ACQUA PAZZA AL LIMONE CON VERDURINE

Sea bass fillets in lemon 'crazy water' with vegetables

I dedicate this dish to my friends at Giardiniello restaurant in Minori, who cook fillets of white fish in this way using olive oil, lemon juice and water. The term 'crazy water' is often given to southern Italian fish dishes cooked in water, such as this one. This recipe is simple and very quick to prepare, but you can also get it wrong. The secret to this dish is to keep the pan moving and not stir-fry the veggies or the fish. If easier, lift the pan slightly off the hob, but still touching the gas flame, and keep moving it – this way the veggies and fish will cook through delicately as well as imparting the lemon flavour, and the liquid will thicken very slightly. Serve with some good bread to mop up the delicious sauce.

Serves 2
2 sea bass fillets (approx. 180g/6¼oz total weight)
6 tbsp extra virgin olive oil
80ml (2½fl oz) lemon juice
½ celery stick, cut into thin matchsticks
½ carrot, cut into thin matchsticks
½ courgette, cut into matchsticks (green part only)
¼ red onion, thinly sliced
sea salt and freshly ground black pepper
flat-leaf parsley sprigs, micro leaves and lemon to garnish (optional)

Slice the sea bass fillets in half and set aside.

Put the extra virgin olive oil, lemon juice and a little salt and pepper in a frying pan over a medium heat. Add all the vegetables and cook for a couple of minutes, shaking the pan from time to time. Remove the vegetables with a slotted spoon and arrange on a serving dish.

Put the pan back on the heat and add 8 tablespoons of water. Place the fish fillets in the pan and cook on each side for a couple of minutes, shaking the pan but being careful not to break the fish. Carefully remove the fish and arrange over the vegetables on the serving platter.

Place the pan, with its cooking liquid, back on the heat, shaking it for a few seconds, then pour the sauce over the fish and vegetables, garnish, if desired, and serve immediately.

ORATA AL LIMONE AL CARTOCCIO

Steam-baked lemon-infused sea bream

I love cooking fish *al cartoccio* (steam-baked), which is not only a healthy way of cooking, but the parcel seals in all the flavours (and saves on washing up!). Ask your fishmonger to clean the sea bream and make a slit down its belly so you can fill the cavity. The subtle lemon flavour really comes out and, for an added kick, I like to serve this dish with Sicilian Dressing (see page 184).

Serves 2
1 whole sea bream, weighing approx. 460g (1lb)
1 garlic clove, finely chopped
handful of flat-leaf parsley, roughly chopped, plus extra sprigs
leaves of 2 thyme sprigs, plus an extra sprig
¼ red chilli, finely chopped
1 tbsp extra virgin olive oil, plus extra for drizzling
zest and juice of ½ unwaxed lemon, plus 3 lemon
    slices, halved (depending on the size; if using
    small lemons, keep the slices whole)
sea salt

Preheat the oven to 160°C fan/180°C/gas mark 4.

Rinse the sea bream under cold running water, then pat dry with kitchen paper or a tea towel. Place the fish on a large piece of parchment paper, which is in turn placed on top of a large piece of aluminium foil.

Combine the garlic, parsley, thyme leaves, chilli, extra virgin olive oil and lemon zest and juice and fill the cavity of the sea bream with this mixture, followed by a couple of lemon halves. Sprinkle the fish all over with salt, place the remaining lemon slices on top with the parsley and thyme sprigs and drizzle all over with extra virgin olive oil. Then wrap tightly in the foil, place on a flat baking tray and bake in the oven for 40 minutes.

Remove from the oven, carefully unwrap the parcel and serve the fish with Sicilian Dressing (page 184), if desired.

MERLUZZO CON CROSTA DI ERBE MISTE E LIMONE

Cod fillets with a mixed herb and lemon crust

This delicious and simple fish dish is quick and easy to prepare and makes a lovely meal for any day of the week. The lemon juice enhances the breadcrumb coating and complements the fish fillets perfectly. I have used cod, but hake is just as good. Serve with some boiled new potatoes and a green salad.

Serves 4
4 cod fillets, weighing approx. 200g (7oz) each
extra virgin olive oil
lemon wedges, to serve

For the crust
100g (3½oz) bread (crusts removed)
2 small thyme sprigs, leaves stripped
a small handful of flat-leaf parsley
1 rosemary sprig, needles stripped
15g (½oz) capers
1 garlic clove
2 anchovy fillets
juice of ½ lemon
1 tbsp extra virgin olive oil
sea salt and freshly ground black pepper

Preheat the oven to 200°C fan/220°C/gas mark 7.

Place all the crust ingredients in a blender and whizz until fairly smooth. Set aside.

Pat dry the fish fillets using kitchen paper to ensure there is no moisture. Rub a little salt and pepper all over the fillets, then a little extra virgin olive oil. Place a non-stick frying pan, preferably ovenproof, over a medium heat, place the fish skin-side down and fry for a minute or so, then turn over carefully and fry for another couple of minutes on the other side. Remove from the heat – if your pan is not ovenproof, carefully transfer the fish into an ovenproof dish. Top each fillet with the breadcrumb mixture and place in the hot oven for 8 minutes until the crust is golden. Remove from the oven and serve immediately with lemon wedges.

INVOLTINI DI SOGLIOLA AL FORNO

Baked rolled sole fillets

Sole is a delicately flavoured fish, which is perfectly enhanced with this subtle paste of capers, anchovies, parsley and lemon. Make sure you cover the dish with foil for the first 10 minutes so the fish inside can steam-cook nicely. Serve 2 involtini per person accompanied by Sautéed Green Beans (see page 74) or Lemon-marinated Courgettes (see page 84), or a simple green salad for a lovely, light and healthy main course.

Serves 2
2 sole fillets, weighing approx. 150g (5½oz) each
breadcrumbs, to sprinkle
extra virgin olive oil
4 large bay leaves
4 slices of lemon
sea salt and freshly ground black pepper

For the filling
15g (½oz) capers, finely chopped
3 anchovy fillets, finely chopped
½ garlic clove, finely chopped
zest of ½ unwaxed lemon
½ handful of flat-leaf parsley leaves, finely chopped
2 tsp extra virgin olive oil

Preheat the oven to 160°C fan/180°C/gas mark 4.

Cut the sole fillets in half lengthways so you end up with four long pieces. Place each one skin-side down with the widest part nearest to you.

Combine all the filling ingredients and spread over the sole fillets, then sprinkle with breadcrumbs and carefully roll the fillets up, starting with the wider part.

Drizzle the base of an ovenproof dish with a little extra virgin olive oil, then lay the bay leaves in the dish topped with a lemon slice. Place a sole involtino over each lemon slice, seam-side down. Sprinkle the fish with salt and pepper and drizzle with extra virgin olive oil.

Cover with foil and bake in the oven for 20 minutes, removing the foil halfway through. Remove from the oven and serve immediately.

SARDINE RIPIENE

Filled sardines coated in breadcrumbs

This recipe is inspired by a similar one made by the chef of my favourite restaurant, Giardiniello, in Minori, who uses anchovies freshly caught off the Amalfi Coast and fills them with the local Provola cheese. Since fresh anchovies are not readily available in the UK, I decided to use sardines and fill them with a tuna and lemon filling. If you are able to get fresh anchovies, by all means use them, but as they are smaller you will probably need to use two anchovies at a time and sandwich them together with the filling. If you can't get either fish or just like the taste of the filling, you can make the filling mixture into delicious *polpettine* (see page 42).

Serves 4

12 headless sardines, cleaned and butterflied
3 eggs, beaten with a little salt
breadcrumbs, for coating
vegetable or sunflower oil, for shallow frying
lemon wedges, to serve

For the filling

120g (4oz) tinned tuna (drained weight)
60g (2¼oz) ricotta cheese
2 tsp finely chopped flat-leaf parsley
2 anchovy fillets, finely chopped
10g (¼oz) capers, finely chopped
10g (¼oz) grated Parmesan cheese
zest of 1 unwaxed lemon and 5 tsp lemon juice

First make the filling. Combine all the ingredients to make a smooth, but not runny mixture and set aside.

Prepare two bowls, one with the beaten eggs and the other with lots of breadcrumbs in it and set aside.

Pat dry the sardines with kitchen paper and lay them flat on a board or work surface, skin-side down. Place some filling in each cavity and close the sardine – don't worry if the filling is showing as it will be covered by breadcrumbs. Dip the filled sardines in beaten egg then coat well in breadcrumbs.

Heat enough oil to cover the base of a large frying pan. When hot, lower in the sardines, filling-side down, and fry for a minute or so and then turn over with the aid of a pair of tongs and continue to fry until golden all over. Remove from the heat and drain on kitchen paper. Serve immediately with lemon wedges.

TRANCI DI SALMONE AL FORNO CON FINOCCHIO E AGRUMI

Baked salmon steaks with fennel, orange and lemon

Fish, fennel and citrus fruits go so well together. This delicate salmon dish is simple to prepare and makes a tasty meal served with perhaps a green salad. Salmon steaks are quite large so it's up to you whether you want to serve a whole one per person or share it between two. If you prefer, you could make this with salmon fillets and if so, reduce the cooking time by about 7–10 minutes.

Serves 2–4
1 fennel bulb, sliced, green fronds reserved
2 large salmon steaks, weighing approx. 300g (3½oz) each
a little extra virgin olive oil
6 thin lemon slices
6 thin orange slices
squeeze of lemon juice
a few flat-leaf parsley leaves
sea salt and freshly ground black pepper
breadcrumbs, for sprinkling

Preheat the oven to 160°C fan/ 180°C /gas mark 4.

Put the fennel slices in a pan of boiling water and blanch for a couple of minutes. Drain well and set aside.

Lightly grease an ovenproof dish with a little extra virgin olive oil, then line with the lemon and orange slices. Place the salmon steaks on top, sprinkle with salt and pepper, drizzle with a little lemon juice, scatter over some parsley, top with the green fennel fronds and fennel slices and a scatting of salt and pepper. Sprinkle the breadcrumbs all over and bake in the oven for about 25 minutes until the fish is cooked through.

Remove from the oven and serve immediately.

MERLUZZO AL BURRO E LIMONE

Hake with butter and lemon

The combination of butter, lemon and capers with white fish is perfect. Very simple and quick to prepare, this light fish dish can be served with some boiled baby potatoes and Sautéed Green Beans (see page 74). If you prefer you can use cod, fillets of sea bass or sea bream or other white fish.

Serves 4
4 hake fillets, weighing approx. 600g (1lb 5oz) in total
100g (3½oz) butter
3 anchovy fillets, finely chopped
2 tbsp capers
zest of ½ unwaxed lemon and 4 tbsp juice
8 mint leaves, finely chopped
sea salt and freshly ground black pepper

Season the hake all over with salt and pepper.

Melt 40g (1½oz) of the butter in a large frying pan over a medium heat, add the anchovy fillets and cook for a minute or so until they dissolve. Add the hake fillets and cook for a couple of minutes on each side, then place skin-side down. Add the capers, half the lemon juice, 30g (1oz) of the butter and half the mint and continue to cook for 2–3 minutes until the hake is cooked through.

Transfer the hake to a serving dish, add the remaining butter to the pan, increase the heat, stir in the remaining lemon juice and pour over the fish. Sprinkle with the lemon zest and remaining mint and serve immediately.

MEAT

PICCATINA AL LIMONE

Veal escalopes with butter and lemon

This classic meat dish has always been a favourite on Italian menus the world over. It can also be made with pork or chicken escalopes. Serve with boiled baby potatoes and lemony carrots for a quick and delicious meal.

Serves 4
400g (14oz) veal escalopes, thinly sliced
flour, for dusting
80g (2¾oz) butter
5 sage leaves
zest and juice of 1 unwaxed lemon
75ml (2½fl oz) white wine
sea salt and freshly ground black pepper
lemon wedges, to serve

For the carrots
8 medium carrots
2 tbsp extra virgin olive oil
juice of ½ lemon
½ handful of flat-leaf parsley, roughly chopped

Dust the meat in flour, shaking off the excess.

For the carrots, cook them in boiling water until nearly tender. Drain and add to a frying pan with the olive oil and sauté for about 4 minutes. Add the lemon juice and parsley and keep warm to serve with the veal.

Melt the butter in a large frying pan and add the sage leaves. Add the veal slices and fry over a medium heat for about 3 minutes on each side.

Pour in the lemon juice and white wine and, shaking the pan, allow to evaporate gently until the sauce has reduced by half and has a creamy consistency. Remove from the heat, season with salt and pepper to taste and serve immediately with lemon zest and wedges of lemon.

INVOLTINI DI POLLO ALLA SICILIANA

Sicilian-style chicken involtini

These delicious chicken rolls are filled with typically Sicilian ingredients of pistachios and citrus fruits. The addition of salami gives the filling an extra kick – try to get a whole piece of salami as opposed to slices, so you cut it into small cubes. I suggest a plain pork salami, such as Milano or Napoli. If you prefer, you could substitute the chicken with pork or veal escalopes, pounding them well to get thin slices. Sometimes, I like to add onions, red peppers and courgettes to the skewers too, along with some lemon leaves to add flavour.

Makes approx. 8 involtini/Serves 4
500g (1lb 2oz) chicken breast, sliced horizontally
    into about 8 thin escalopes
extra virgin olive oil
breadcrumbs
sea salt and freshly ground black pepper

For the filling
100g (3½oz) bread, crusts removed
35g (1¼oz) grated Parmesan cheese
20g (¾oz) pistachios, finely chopped
65g (2¼oz) salami, chopped into small cubes
zest and juice of ½ unwaxed orange
zest and juice of ½ unwaxed lemon

Preheat the oven to 160°C fan/180°C/gas mark 4 and lightly grease a baking tray.

Place the chicken breasts on a large board or work surface, sprinkle with a little salt and pepper and rub with extra virgin olive oil all over.

Combine all the filling ingredients, including some black pepper and enough extra virgin olive oil to make the filling stick together – a bit like dough. Divide the filling into eight pieces, form into small sausage shapes, then place on the chicken and roll up to enclose the filling. Secure with toothpicks or wooden skewers.

Place the involtini on the baking tray, sprinkle with breadcrumbs, drizzle with extra virgin olive oil and bake in the oven for 25 minutes. Insert the tip of a sharp knife to check that the chicken is cooked through. Remove from the oven and serve immediately.

POLLO ARROSTO CON ERBE AL PROFUMO DI LIMONE

Lemon and herb-infused roast chicken with lemon gravy

I always like to add a buttery paste on the chicken flesh underneath the skin to keep it nice and moist during cooking and to add flavour. You can use this same recipe to liven up roast turkey, capon and guinea fowl. The lemon and herb flavours really come through, making this a tasty Sunday lunch. When making the gravy with the roasting juices, I like to add lemon juice for an extra lemony hit. The flavour is not overpowering; in fact lemon combines so well with the herbs and juices from the roast chicken, you will always want to cook roast chicken this way! Serve with roast potatoes.

Serves 4

1.6kg (3lb 8oz) free-range organic chicken
handful of mixed fresh herbs – rosemary sprigs, thyme sprigs,
    bay leaves and sage leaves – tied in a bunch
2 large carrots, halved lengthways
2 large leeks, halved lengthways
extra virgin olive oil, for drizzling
200ml (7fl oz) white wine
5ml (2fl oz) water
juice of ½ lemon
2 tsp plain flour
sea salt and freshly ground black pepper

For the lemon and herb butter

150g (5½oz) butter, softened at room temperature
needles from 2 rosemary sprigs, finely chopped
leaves from 4 thyme sprigs
6 sage leaves, finely chopped
1 garlic clove, finely chopped
zest of 2 unwaxed lemons and juice of 1 lemon –
    reserve two of the lemon halves

Preheat the oven to 200°C fan/220°C/gas mark 7.

Combine all the ingredients for the herb butter until you obtain a smooth paste.

continued on next page...

Take the chicken and, starting at the neck end, gently ease the skin of the chicken away from the breast, taking care not to tear the delicate skin. Using your fingers, spread three-quarters of the paste as evenly as possible under the skin all over the breast and thighs, then gently pat the skin to even out the paste. Next, fill the chicken cavity with the two reserved lemon halves and bunch of mixed herbs.

Line a roasting tin with the carrots and leeks and drizzle with a little extra virgin olive oil. Place the chicken on top of the vegetables – this will prevent the chicken from sticking to the tin. Season the chicken all over with some salt and pepper, drizzle with a little extra virgin olive oil, rubbing well all over. Pour in the wine and water and cover with foil.

Reduce the oven temperature to 180°C fan/200°C/gas mark 6 and roast the chicken for about 1 hour 30–40 minutes, removing the foil for the last 30 minutes, until cooked through. During cooking, baste the chicken with the juices from time to time.

Remove the roasting tin from the oven and immediately place the remaining butter on top of the chicken to melt, using a spatula to spread it all over. Carefully remove the chicken and vegetables, place on a board and leave to rest for about 10 minutes before carving.

In the meantime, make the gravy. Combine the juices left in the roasting tin with the juice of ½ lemon, about 200ml (7fl oz) of water and place over a high heat, whisk in the flour and continue mixing until the gravy has thickened slightly. Strain, pour into a jug and serve with the roast chicken and vegetables.

CONIGLIO AL FORNO DI ERMINIA CON LE FOGLIE DI LIMONE

Erminia's recipe for rabbit baked in lemon leaves

This traditional recipe is from the village of Conca dei Marini on the Amalfi Coast. It was given to my sister, Adriana, by her friend Erminia, who originates from the village. An abundance of fresh lemon leaves is used to slow-roast chunks of rabbit which have been coated in a delicious breadcrumb mixture. The delicate rabbit meat is subtly flavoured by the essential oil exuded from the lemon leaves during cooking. If you are unable to get lemon leaves, you can still make this recipe using lemon slices. Either way, it's delicious served with a mixed salad and the Lemon Salsa Verde (see page 185) or Lemon Mayo (see page 182)

Serves 4–6

1.2kg (2lb 10oz) rabbit, unboned and cut into chunks
zest and juice of 1 unwaxed lemon
approx. 100g (3½oz) breadcrumbs
50g (1¾oz) grated Pecorino cheese
a small handful of flat-leaf parsley leaves, finely chopped
1 rosemary sprig, needles stripped and finely chopped
1 large garlic clove, very finely chopped
extra virgin olive oil
vegetable or sunflower oil, for greasing
abundant lemon leaves, or 2 lemons, sliced thinly
sea salt

Rinse the rabbit chunks under cold running water and pat dry on kitchen paper. Place in a large bowl, drizzle over the lemon juice and add enough water to cover teh meat. Cover and set aside for a couple of hours – in hot weather, place in the fridge.

Preheat the oven to 170°C fan/190°C/gas mark 5.

Combine the breadcrumbs, Pecorino, parsley, rosemary, garlic and lemon zest.

Drain the rabbit well and rub salt and extra virgin olive oil all over each piece, then coat in the breadcrumb mixture.

Grease a large roasting tin with some oil and line the base with slightly overlapping lemon leaves so that the base is covered.

continued on next page...

Place the breadcrumbed rabbit chunks on top, cover with more lemon leaves and drizzle with some oil.

Place in the oven for 90 minutes. Halfway through the cooking time, remove the tin, turn over the rabbit chunks and place more fresh lemon leaves over the top. At the end of cooking time, increase the heat to 200°C fan/220°C/gas mark 7, discard the top leaves and continue to cook for about 5 minutes until the rabbit is golden. Remove from the oven and serve.

Alternative method using fresh lemon slices
Line the roasting tin with lemon slices, place the rabbit chunks on top and cover with more lemon slices. Follow the method as above.

AGNELLO PASQUALE CON UOVA E LIMONE

Easter lamb with eggs and lemon

This traditional lamb dish is popular in central and southern Italy during Easter and spring when lamb is at its best and eggs are celebrated. The tangy taste of lemon gives a kick to the lamb, balancing its often strong flavour. Serve with good bread to mop up the sauce and Sautéed Green Beans (see page 74) or a green salad.

Serves 4
3 tbsp extra virgin olive oil
1 onion, finely sliced
1 garlic clove, finely chopped
1 rosemary sprig, plus ½ sprig, needles stripped
    and finely chopped
1kg (2lb 4oz) lamb shoulder, boned and cut into chunks
juice and zest of 2 unwaxed lemons
150ml (5fl oz) vegetable stock
2 eggs
40g (1¼oz) grated Pecorino cheese
rosemary needles from ½ sprig, finely chopped
sea salt and freshly ground black pepper

Heat the extra virgin olive oil in a large saucepan, add the onion and sweat on a medium heat for 2–3 minutes until softened. Add the garlic and the rosemary sprig and continue to sweat for a minute. Add the lamb, increase the heat and seal well on all sides. Pour in the lemon juice and stock, reduce the heat, cover with a lid and cook gently for 1½ hours until the lamb is tender.

Near the end of cooking time, combine the eggs, pecorino, chopped rosemary, lemon zest and some salt and pepper.

Remove the pan from the heat and gradually stir in the egg mixture until you obtain a creamy sauce. Make sure the eggs don't scramble. Serve immediately.

Tip
If you plan to serve this later, add the egg mixture just before serving.

LEPRE AL LIMONE CON PATATE E MELE

Lemon-infused hare with potatoes and apples

Lemon and apple lend a lovely sweet and sour flavour to hare, which is a meat I love. We would often have hare in Italy and it was always soaked in water and lemon juice to remove any impurities and reduce its strong gamey flavour. If you prefer, you can make this rustic dish using rabbit or chicken instead.

Serves 4–6

1.2kg (2lb 12oz) prepared hare, on the bone
   but cut into chunks
zest and juice of 1 unwaxed lemon, the two halves reserved
3 apples, cored and sliced into thick rings
120ml (4fl oz) lemon juice (from about 2 large lemons),
   plus extra for drizzling
4 tbsp extra virgin olive oil
3 rosemary sprigs
100ml (3½fl oz) white wine
800ml (28fl oz) vegetable stock
750g (1lb 10oz) potatoes, peeled and cut into chunks
60g (2¼oz) butter
sea salt and freshly ground black pepper

Place the hare chunks in a bowl, cover with fresh cold water, add the juice of 1 lemon plus the squeezed lemon halves and leave to soak for about 20 minutes.

Drizzle the apple rings with 120ml (4fl oz) of lemon juice and set aside.

Drain the hare chunks, pat dry with kitchen paper and season all over with salt and pepper.

Heat the extra virgin olive oil in a large pan, add the rosemary and sweat for a minute over a medium heat. Add the hare chunks and seal well on all sides. Drain the lemon juice from the apples (set them to one side) and add it to the pan with the white wine and allow to evaporate slightly. Add the stock, bring to the boil, then reduce the heat, cover with a lid and cook for about 50 minutes until the meat is tender. About halfway through, add the potatoes.

Towards the end of cooking time, melt the butter in a frying pan, add the apple rings and caramelize them on both sides. Place on a large serving dish with the hare and potatoes and sprinkle with the lemon zest. Serve immediately with a drizzle of lemon juice, if desired.

ARROSTO DI MAIALE AL LIMONE SERVITO CON SPINACI

Rolled roast loin of pork served with spinach

This dish makes a great light Sunday lunch. Ask your butcher to butterfly the pork loin for you to make it easier and quicker to prepare. I have used *cipolotti*, which are fat spring onions, but you can equally use regular ones. The pork can be eaten hot or cold – in fact it's more delicious the following day once all the flavours have infused, enhancing the lemon and rosemary taste.

Serves 6
pared rind of 2 unwaxed lemons
1 tsp sugar
2 tbsp extra virgin olive oil, plus extra for drizzling
6 rosemary sprigs
200g (7oz) *cipolotti* (or regular spring onions) – trimmed weight (just
    trim off the roots)
1kg (2lb 4oz) pork loin – cut into a long piece
    ready for rolling
150ml (5fl oz) white wine
sea salt and freshly ground black pepper

for the spinach
2 tbsp extra virgin olive oil
4 whole, unpeeled garlic cloves
200g (7oz) baby spinach
sea salt
juice of 1 lemon (see above)

Preheat the oven to 180°C fan/200°C/gas mark 6.

Put the lemon rind with the sugar and enough water to cover in a small pan, bring to the boil and boil for 10 minutes. Drain off the water, pat the rind dry and set aside.

Heat 2 tablespoons of extra virgin olive oil in a frying pan large enough to accommodate the loin of pork. Add the rosemary and *cipolotti* and gently stir-fry for about 7 minutes (less if you are using regular spring onions) until golden and slightly softened. Remove from the heat and set aside.

continued on next page...

Unroll the pork loin, place on a flat surface skin-side down, flattening it slightly with a meat tenderizer. Drizzle with a little extra virgin olive oil, sprinkle with salt, pepper and the needles from two of the rosemary sprigs. Slice three-quarters of the cipolotti in two lengthways (if using spring onions keep whole) and place on the pork loin together with three-quarters of the lemon peel. Roll the pork up and tie tightly with kitchen string.

Replace the frying pan on the heat (it will still contain olive oil and the remaining rosemary). Seal the pork joint on all sides. Pour in the white wine and allow to evaporate slightly. Remove from the heat.

Drizzle a little extra virgin olive oil in a roasting tin, place the remaining cipolotti or spring onions on the bottom of the roasting dish with the remaining sprigs of rosemary. Place the pork on top, drizzle with a little extra virgin olive oil, pour over the juices from the frying pan, cover with foil and roast in the oven for about 1 hour, basting from time to time. If necessary, add a little hot water to the roasting tin during cooking to prevent it drying out. Remove the foil for the last 15 minutes.

Remove from the oven, leave to rest for 5–10 minutes, pour the juices into a jug and keep warm.

Meanwhile, prepare the spinach. Heat the extra virgin olive oil in a frying pan, add the garlic cloves and sweat over a medium heat for 3 minutes. Add the spinach, a little salt and stir-fry for a couple of minutes until wilted. Remove from the pan and drizzle with lemon juice.

Slice the pork, garnish with the remaining lemon rind and serve with the juices and spinach.

BURGER DI TACCHINO AL PROFUMO DI LIMONE

Lemon-infused turkey burgers

For a lighter, healthier burger, try these turkey mince burgers with a delicious hint of herbs and lemon as an alternative to the usual beef. Enjoy them by themselves accompanied with Roasted Pepper Salad (see page 45) or in a bun with some Lemon Mayo (see page 182).

Makes 6 burgers
50g (1¾oz) stale bread, soaked in a little warm water
400g (14oz) minced turkey
2 garlic cloves, finely chopped
1 rosemary sprig, needles stripped and finely chopped
2 thyme sprigs, leaves stripped and finely chopped
30g (1oz) grated Parmesan cheese
zest and juice of 1 unwaxed lemon, plus extra zest to serve (optional)
1 egg
plain flour, for dusting
2–3 tbsp extra virgin olive oil
4 tbsp water
sea salt and freshly ground black pepper

To serve (optional)
6 burger buns
Lemon Mayo (see page 182)
a large handful of rocket leaves
Parmesan shavings
grated lemon zest

Remove the bread from the water, use your hands to squeeze out the excess liquid and then finely chop. Combine the minced turkey, bread, garlic, herbs, Parmesan, lemon zest, egg and some salt and pepper. Divide the mixture into six, shape into burger patties and lightly dust with flour.

Heat the olive oil in a large frying pan and, when hot, add the burgers and fry over a high heat for 2–3 minutes on each side until golden and a slight crust has formed. Combine the lemon juice and water, pour over, cover with a lid, reduce the heat to medium and cook for about 2 minutes until the liquid has been absorbed. Remove from the heat and serve immediately with extra lemon zest, if desired.

Or, if you are serving in a bun, serve with lemon mayo, a little rocket, Parmesan shavings and freshly grated lemon zest.

DESSERTS

SORBETTO AL LIMONE E MENTA
Lemon and mint sorbet

This tangy refreshing sorbet is perfect on hot summer days but it's just as enjoyable during winter. Serve with mixed berries for a refreshing dessert with some Lemon Biscuits (see page 136).

Serves 4–6
4 unwaxed lemons
approx. 30 mint leaves, plus extra to decorate
250g (9oz) caster sugar
500ml (18fl oz) water

Finely pare the rind from two of the lemons, trying to avoid the white pith as much as possible, and grate the other two using a zester. Then halve and juice all four lemons. Finely chop half the mint.

Place the lemon rind, sugar, water and whole mint leaves in a pan over a high heat and bring to the boil, stirring from time to time. Continue to boil for 7 minutes, then remove from the heat and allow to cool.

When cool, discard the rind (or reserve for decoration) and mint. Combine the liquid with the lemon zest and finely chopped mint. Pour into a lidded freezerproof container and place in the freezer for about 4–5 hours. Every hour or so, give the sorbet a good stir with a small whisk to break up the ice crystals.

Remove from the freezer and leave at room temperature for about 20 minutes before serving. Decorate with the lemon rind and extra fresh mint leaves, if desired.

BISCOTTI MORBIDI AL LIMONE

Lemon biscuits

These deliciously soft biscuits with the aromatic hint of lemon are really addictive. When we tested them for this book, we began eating them straight from the oven and their lovely home-baked aroma filled the house. If you can keep them for longer, they will keep for about a week in an airtight container. You can also make them with orange or combine both for a delicious citrussy flavour.

Makes approx. 25 biscuits

100g (3½oz) butter, softened at room temperature
80g (2¾oz) caster sugar, plus extra for coating
1 egg, lightly beaten
zest and juice of 1 unwaxed lemon
300g (10½oz) self-raising flour, sifted
abundant icing sugar, for coating

Line a large flat baking tray with baking paper.

Beat the butter and sugar until creamy, gradually beat in the egg and combine well together. Stir in the lemon zest and juice and gradually add the flour until it is all incorporated and forms a soft dough. Shape into a ball, wrap in clingfilm and leave to rest in the fridge for 1 hour.

Meanwhile, preheat the oven to 160°C fan/180°C/gas mark 4.

Take two plates and scatter the extra caster sugar on one and sifted icing sugar on the other.

Remove the biscuit dough from the fridge and unwrap from the clingfilm. Take small pieces of dough and, with your hands, form small balls the size of a walnut. Roll in the caster sugar and then in the icing sugar, coating well all over. Place on the prepared baking tray (no need to flatten).

Bake in the oven for about 12 minutes until they are just beginning to turn slightly golden and cracks form on the top. Remove from the oven and enjoy!

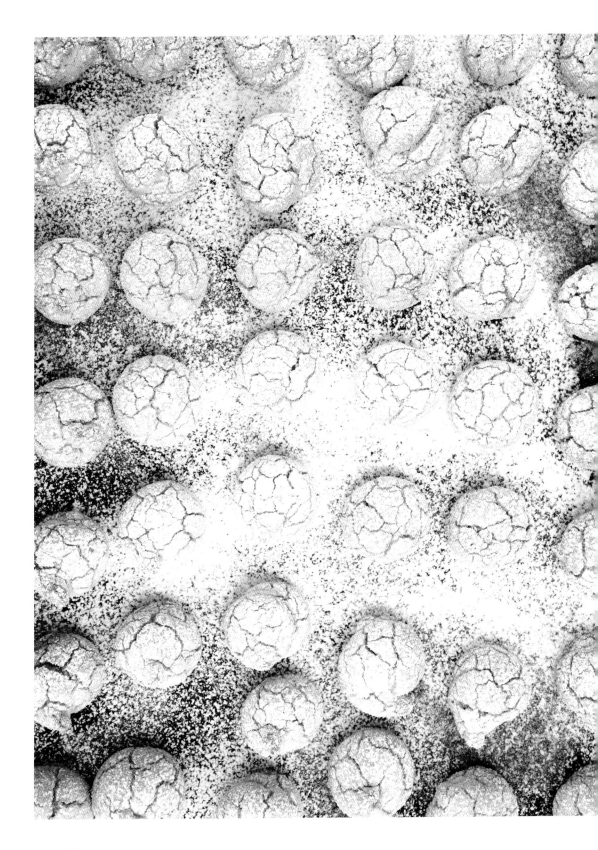

139   Desserts

TORTA DELIZIA AL LIMONE
Creamy lemon cake

This cake is a twist on the classic *Delizia al Limone*, the individual dome-shaped sponge cakes filled and covered with lemon cream that are so popular in pastry shops along the Amalfi Coast. It's really quite simple to make yet it looks really effective – perfect for a special occasion. For the lemon concentrate, I use my Lemon Concentrate recipe (see page 174). Otherwise, use lemon extract.

Serves 8

For the sponge
5 free-range eggs
70g (2½oz) caster sugar
zest of ½ unwaxed lemon
2 tsp Lemon Concentrate (see page 174) or extract
70ml (2½fl oz) mild olive oil
50g (1¾oz) plain flour

For the cream
500ml (18fl oz) double cream
250ml (8½fl oz) natural yogurt
zest of ½ unwaxed lemon
3 tsp Lemon Concentrate or extract
60g (2¼oz) icing sugar, sifted

For the limoncello syrup
2 tsp limoncello (see page 166 for homemade)
2 tsp water
1 tsp caster sugar

To decorate
1 lemon, sliced thinly into half moons
fresh mint leaves

Preheat the oven to 160°C fan/180°C/gas mark 4 and lightly grease a baking tin, approx. 36 x 36cm (14 x 14in) – or you could use a large Swiss roll tin, a roasting tin or the fat tray from your oven/grill. Line with baking parchment.

Separate the eggs into large bowls. Lightly beat the yolks and set aside. Whisk the whites until stiff, then fold in the caster sugar, lemon zest and lemon concentrate.

continued on next page...

Gradually fold in the egg yolks, followed by the oil and then sift in the flour. Pour into the prepared baking tin and bake in the oven for 10–12 minutes until golden.

Meanwhile, make the lemon cream. Whip the cream until stiff and combine with the yogurt, lemon zest, lemon concentrate and sift in the icing sugar.

Remove the sponge from the oven, turn out onto a wire rack and allow to cool before carefully removing the baking parchment. Place on a board or work surface lined with a clean sheet of baking parchment and cut into nine 4-cm (1½-in) strips – keep the strips together for now.

Put the ingredients for the syrup in a small saucepan over a medium heat and stir until the sugar dissolves. Remove from the heat and brush the hot liquid all over the strips.

Once absorbed, spread some of the cream on the first strip and carefully roll it up. Place the roll upright in the centre of a serving plate. Spread cream on the second strip and roll it around the ready-rolled strip on the plate. Continue doing this until you have used up all the strips.

Cover the whole cake with the remaining cream – you could also put some cream in a piping bag and decorate the cake if you wish. Decorate with lemon slices and fresh mint. Place in the fridge for a couple of hours before serving.

FRAGOLE AL LIMONE E BASILICO

Strawberries with lemon and basil

In Italy, strawberries are often combined with lemon juice. This is a perfect light and healthy dessert in summer when ripe sweet strawberries are in season. You may want to add a little more or less sugar depending on how sweet your fruit is. Serve these with Lemon and Mint Sorbet (see page 134), Espresso Coffee and Lemon Semifreddo (page 149) or Parmesan and Lemon Ice Cream (page 148), or simply on their own.

Serves 4
400g (14oz) strawberries, washed, patted dry and hulled
2 tablespoons white wine
zest and juice of 1 unwaxed lemon, plus extra zest
    for sprinkling
6 large basil leaves, roughly torn
75g (2¾oz) icing sugar, sifted

Combine the strawberries, white wine, lemon zest and half the basil leaves in a bowl.

Mix the lemon juice and icing sugar together until the sugar dissolves. Pour over the strawberries, cover and leave to macerate for about 30 minutes. Serve with the remaining basil leaves and a sprinkling of lemon zest.

CROSTATA AL LIMONE

Lemon tart

I love an Italian crostata like this one with its lattice of pastry strips over the filling. It reminds me of home and childhood when we would often have a slice for *merenda* (afternoon snack). This lemon version makes a perfect dessert on its own or served with mixed berries. Adding zest to the pastry really enhances the lemon flavour.

Serves 8
1 x quantity Lemon Custard (see page 188)
egg wash, made with 1 beaten yolk and 1 tbsp milk

For the pastry
250g (9oz) plain flour
125g (4½oz) hard butter, cut into small pieces
75g (2½oz) icing sugar, plus extra to serve
zest of 1 unwaxed lemon
3 egg yolks, lightly beaten

First make the pastry. Sift the flour into a large bowl, add the butter and use your fingers to rub the butter into the flour until the mixture resembles breadcrumbs. Sift in the icing sugar and add the lemon zest. Gradually stir in the egg yolks, then mix well with your hands to form a smooth dough. Form into a ball, wrap in clingfilm and place in the fridge to rest for at least 30 minutes.

Meanwhile, make the custard. Pour into a bowl, cover and leave it to cool.

Preheat the oven to 170°C fan/190°C/gas mark 5. Grease and lightly flour a 22-cm (8½-in) round tart tin.

Unwrap the pastry and transfer to a lightly floured work surface. Roll out to about 5mm (¼in) thick and use to line the prepared tart tin, saving the trimmings. Lightly prick the base with a fork, then pour in the cooled custard.

Gather together, then re-roll the pastry trimmings and cut into strips. Arrange over the top to form a lattice pattern. Brush the strips with a little egg wash.

Transfer the tart to the preheated oven, reduce the temperature to 150°C fan/170°C/ gas mark 3½ and bake for 50 minutes, covering with a loose piece of foil after the first 20 minutes to prevent the custard from browning.

Remove from the oven, leave to cool completely in the tin, dust with icing sugar and serve.

MOUSSE AL CIOCCOLATO BIANCO E LIMONE CON LAMPONI

White chocolate and lemon mousse with raspberries

This super-easy mousse can be made in no time, requires no cooking and does not contain eggs. The combination of white chocolate, lemon and raspberries is perfect and makes a decadent end to a meal, or you could whip this up to serve at parties. It's quite rich, though, so keep the portions small.

Serves 6
½ tablespoon sugar
150g (5½oz) raspberries
100g (3½oz) white chocolate
250ml (8½fl oz) double cream
zest of 1 unwaxed lemon and juice of ½

To decorate
raspberries
mint leaves
grated lemon zest

Drizzle the sugar over the raspberries and set aside for about 30 minutes.

Break the chocolate into pieces and place in a heatproof bowl over a pan of barely simmering water. Do not let the water come into contact with the bowl. Leave until the chocolate has melted and then set aside to cool.

Meanwhile, whip the cream until thick. Mash the raspberries with a fork.

Add the lemon zest and juice to the cooled chocolate and fold in the whipped cream until everything is well combined.

Line small glasses with a little of the mashed raspberries followed by a dollop of the creamy mixture. Repeat to make a couple more layers, finishing with the creamy mixture. Decorate each with a whole raspberry, mint leaves and lemon zest.

Serve immediately or store in the fridge until required.

GELATO AL PARMIGIANO E LIMONE

Parmesan and lemon ice cream

Experimenting with unusual flavours and combining sweet and savoury in ice cream is becoming increasingly popular in Italy – and Parmesan ice cream can be seen in *gelaterie* (ice cream parlours) up and down the country. Parmesan goes so well with lemon, I thought I would try them together. The combination of slightly salty cheese and tangy lemon is perfect and will surely impress your guests for the perfect dinner party dessert. Simple to make, especially if you have an ice cream machine, but just as easy to make by hand. If you really don't like the idea of adding Parmesan, simply omit it and enjoy a lovely creamy lemon ice cream.

Serves 4–6
3 free-range organic egg yolks
100g (3½oz) caster sugar
200ml (7fl oz) double cream
200ml (7fl oz) milk (whole or semi-skimmed)
pared rind of ½ unwaxed lemon
60g (about 2 ½oz) Parmesan cheese, finely grated
zest of 2 unwaxed lemons and 4 tbsp juice

Place an empty plastic container (900ml or 1½ pints) in the freezer while you prepare the ice cream.

Beat the egg yolks and sugar together until creamy. Put the double cream, milk and lemon rind in a pan and gently bring almost to boiling point. Remove from the heat and beat in the egg mixture. Return the pan to a low heat and gently cook, stirring all the time, for 2 minutes. Remove from the heat, discard the lemon rind, and stir in the Parmesan, lemon juice and lemon zest. Place in an ice-cream machine and churn following your machine instructions. Alternatively, make the ice cream by hand as follows:

Take the container out of the freezer, pour in the mixture and place in the freezer for 30 minutes. After this time, remove the container and beat well, then return to the freezer and repeat after 30 minutes. Leave in the freezer for 2–3 hours until the ice cream has set.

If the ice cream has set too hard, remove from the freezer and leave at room temperature for about 10 minutes to soften before serving.

SEMIFREDDO DI CAFFÈ E LIMONE
Espresso coffee and lemon semifreddo

Semifreddo, which translates as 'half cold' is a type of soft ice cream or frozen mousse. Simple to make, without the need to churn, it is a popular dessert in Italy and is often made with mixed berries or nuts. I love the combination of coffee and lemon – I always put a small piece of lemon rind in my espresso – so I decided to make a semifreddo with the same flavours. The slight tang of lemon makes the espresso coffee taste less bitter. It makes the perfect end to a meal. If you love coffee as much as I do, serve this dessert as an affogato – see below.

Serves 6–8
4 tbsp freshly made espresso coffee
zest of 2 unwaxed lemons and 4 tsp lemon juice
200ml (7fl oz) condensed milk
500ml (18fl oz) double cream
lemon rind and coffee beans, to decorate (optional)

First line a 900g (2lb) loaf tin with clingfilm, allowing it to overlap the sides.

Combine the espresso coffee and lemon juice and leave to cool. Then combine this mixture with the condensed milk and lemon zest. Whisk the double cream until stiff and then fold in the coffee mixture until well incorporated. Pour into the prepared tin, cover the surface with overlapping clingfilm and place in the freezer for about 4 hours. To serve, remove from the freezer, unwrap and tip out onto a plate. Decorate with lemon rind and coffee beans, if using, and leave at room temperature for about 10 minutes, before slicing into portions.

Serving suggestion: serve as an affogato by pouring a serving of freshly made sweetened hot espresso over a slab of the semifreddo.

TIRAMISU AL LIMONE

Lemon tiramisu

Here is a lovely refreshing lemon twist to this classic dessert. Savoiardi (ladyfinger or sponge finger biscuits) are dipped in lemon syrup rather than the usual espresso coffee, and lemon zest and a little limoncello flavour the creamy mascarpone. It's a simple dessert, one which can be made in advance and stored in the fridge, and that will surely please everyone. When peeling the lemon, ensure you remove the pith, otherwise the syrup could taste bitter.

Serves 4–6
2 free-range eggs, separated
80g (2¾oz) caster sugar
250g (8½oz) mascarpone
2 tbsp limoncello (see page 166 for homemade)
zest of 1 unwaxed lemon
200g (7oz) Savoiardi biscuits

For the lemon syrup
rind and juice of 1 unwaxed lemon (white pith removed)
100ml (3½fl oz) water
50g (1¾oz) caster sugar

To make the lemon syrup, place all the ingredients in a small pan over a medium heat and simmer for 3–4 minutes until the sugar has dissolved and the liquid has reduced slightly. Remove from the heat and leave to cool. Take out the lemon peel, finely chop and set aside.

Whisk the egg yolks and sugar together until light and creamy. Add the mascarpone and continue to whisk. Stir in the limoncello and lemon zest. Whisk the egg whites in a separate clean bowl until stiff, then fold into the creamy mixture and combine well together.

Spread a little of the creamy mascarpone mixture on the base of a serving dish. One by one, quickly dip the biscuits into the lemon syrup and put them in the dish to form a layer. Top with more mascarpone and continue to dip the biscuits and build up the layers until the ingredients have been used, ending with a layer of the mascarpone. Sprinkle the finely chopped lemon rind on top and leave in the fridge until required.

DOLCE D'AMALFI

Lemon and almond cake

This cake is the recipe of Salvatore De Riso, a good friend and an excellent pastry chef, from my home village of Minori. He creates the most beautiful cakes, using local ingredients and turning them into edible masterpieces. This wonderfully moist and light cake with the delicate taste of lemon and almonds is very simple to make. It is usually made in a dome shape, but if you don't have a hemisphere cake tin, a regular 20cm (8in) round tin will be fine.

Serves 4–6

130g (4¾oz) butter, softened
160g (5¾oz) icing sugar, sifted
zest of 2 unwaxed lemons
60g (2¼oz) Candied Lemon Peel (see page 158),
    very finely chopped
seeds from ½ vanilla pod
2 large eggs, lightly beaten
130g (4¾oz) plain flour, sifted
1 tsp baking powder, sifted
100g (3½oz) ground almonds
100ml (3½fl oz) milk, at room temperature

To decorate
lemon slices
grated lemon zest
icing sugar

Preheat the oven to 160°C fan/180°C/gas mark 4. Lightly grease an 18cm (7in) hemisphere cake tin (or simply use a 20cm/8in round one) and lightly dust with fine semolina flour.

Cream the butter and icing sugar together until light and fluffy. Add the lemon zest, candied lemon peel and vanilla seeds. Gradually whisk in the eggs. With a metal spoon, fold in the flour, baking powder and ground almonds. Gradually add the milk and stir well. Pour the mixture into the prepared tin and bake for about 45–50 minutes until risen and golden.

Remove from the oven, leave for 5 minutes, then gently turn out onto a plate. When cool, dust with a little icing sugar and decorate with freshly grated lemon zest and a couple of lemon slices, if desired.

ZUPPA INGLESE AL CIOCCOLATO E LIMONE

Chocolate and lemon Italian trifle

Zuppa Inglese has nothing to do with soup as its Italian title suggests, and I am not sure how the name came about, but with the custard and sponge biscuits it is very similar to an English trifle. I use the Italian sponge fingers Savoiardi (ladyfinger or sponge biscuits) in this recipe, but you could use leftover pandoro or a plain sponge cake instead.

Serves 6
6 free-range egg yolks
130g (4¾oz) caster sugar
50g (1¾oz) plain flour, sifted
500ml (18fl oz) hot (not boiling) milk
½ tsp vanilla extract
pared rind of ¼ unwaxed lemon and 4 tsp lemon juice
2 tsp cocoa powder, sifted
200g (7oz) Savoiardi biscuits

For the syrup
200ml (7fl oz) water
25g (1oz) caster sugar
50ml (1¾fl oz) limoncello (see page 166 for homemade)

To decorate
grated dark chocolate
grated lemon zest

For the syrup, put the water and sugar in a pan over a medium heat and stir until the sugar has dissolved. Remove from the heat, pour in the limoncello and set aside.

In a saucepan, whisk together the egg yolks and sugar for about 5 minutes until the sugar has dissolved and the mixture is smooth and creamy. Add the flour and continue to whisk until well amalgamated. Whisk in the hot milk, vanilla extract and lemon rind, then place the pan over a low heat, stirring all the time with the whisk or a wooden spoon, until it thickens. Remove from the heat and pour half the custard into a bowl, discard the lemon rind, and stir in the lemon juice. Add the sifted cocoa powder to the remaining custard and mix well until combined.

Dip the biscuits into the syrup and use to line a glass serving bowl. Spoon over a layer of the chocolate custard, then lay more biscuits on top, then a layer of lemon custard. Continue making these layers, finishing with the lemon custard. Decorate with grated chocolate and lemon zest. Store in the fridge until required.

LIMONI CANDITI

Candied lemon

When I went to Italy to shoot this book, my friends at Pasticceria Gambardella were making candied lemon and orange peel to sell in their shop. Homemade candied peel is so much tastier (and healthier) than the sugary sticky shop-bought variety. The strips of peel can be chopped up and used in cakes or desserts, dipped in chocolate or eaten as they are for a sweet treat. You can also use oranges and clementines for this recipe. Whatever weight of peel you obtain, you need equal amounts of sugar and water. Don't throw away the rest of the lemon: use the juice for dressings, in cooking or to make lemon drinks.

Makes 1 x 340g (11¾oz) jar
peel of 3 unwaxed lemons – about 130g (4¾oz) in weight
    and about 5mm (¼in) in thickness
130g (4¾oz) caster sugar
130ml (4¾fl oz) water

Cut the lemon peel into thick strips. Place in a pan and cover with cold water, bring to the boil and boil rapidly for a couple of minutes. Drain, add fresh water and repeat this process twice.

After the third time, drain and return to the pan with the sugar and measured water, bring to the boil and continue boiling until the liquid has evaporated, but be careful not to let it burn.

Remove from the heat, and use a pair of tongs to remove the peel and place on a wire rack over a large dish or tray to catch the excess liquid. Leave to dry out for 2–3 days.

Place in an airtight container and use as candied peel or for decoration as required. Or dip into melted dark chocolate, allow to dry and enjoy as a treat.

DRINKS & PRESERVES

GRANITA AL LIMONE DI PAPA' ANTONIO

Lemon granita

Lemon granita is the best thirst-quencher during long hot summer days. This recipe comes from Papa' Antonio, the late father of Sal De Riso, who used to make lemon granita in his tiny cafe in Minori when I was a little boy. I would often watch him zest the lemons and volunteer to help, as I knew at the end I would be rewarded with a large glass of ice-cold granita. So simple to prepare, it's worth making a large batch, especially during a heatwave, so you always have something refreshing to enjoy. It's also lovely to add to Valentino's Limoncello Spritz (see page 169).

Serves 4–6
200ml (7fl oz) lemon juice
200g (7oz) caster sugar
zest of 2 unwaxed lemons
1.25 litres (about 2¼ pints) very cold water

Strain the lemon juice through a fine sieve into a bowl and add the sugar, stirring until the sugar dissolves. Stir in the cold water and lemon zest. Pour into a container and place in the freezer for 45 minutes. After this time, remove and use a fork to break up the ice crystals. Return to the freezer for 30 minutes and repeat. Do this a couple more times, after which time it should be set, but not hard. Remove and serve in glasses.

If the granita goes too hard, simply leave at room temperature for a few minutes to melt a little and break up the ice crystals with a fork.

LIMONCELLO

This popular after-dinner drink was once only made at home along the Amalfi Coast and Sorrento where lemons grow so plentifully. Nowadays, there are many producers who export this liqueur all over the world. I still like to make my own and enjoy the ritual of placing the lemon rinds in a jar with the alcohol. Try to get pure alcohol, which you can buy online or ask at your Italian deli. As a drink, serve limoncello cold – you can also use it in a variety of desserts.

Makes approx. 1.25 litres (about 2¼ pints)
3 unwaxed lemons
500ml (18fl oz) pure alcohol
750ml (26fl oz) water
400g (14oz) sugar

Wash the lemons in cold water, then dry well. Carefully pare off the lemon rind, making sure you avoid the white pith. Place the rind in a large jar, pour over the alcohol and seal hermetically. Place in a cool, dry place for 7 days.

Put the water in a pan over the heat and bring to the boil, add the sugar and stir until the sugar has dissolved. Remove from the heat and allow to cool.

Open the jar and strain the lemon-infused alcohol through a fine sieve, discarding all the peel. Add the alcohol to the sugared water and mix well together. Leave to cool completely, then pour into clean, dry bottles. Seal with lids and store in a cool, dark place for at least 10 days.

LO SPRITZ DI VALENTINO

Valentino's limoncello spritz

This aperitif idea comes from my friend Valentino, who makes his own limoncello from his little factory in Praiano near Positano. Normally, this spritz is made simply with one part limoncello and topped up with Prosecco, but Valentino also adds one part lemon granita to give it that extra-special refreshing tang. It's an ideal summer aperitif; just make sure you have some lemon granita in the freezer or, if you don't, then simply make it without. And make sure your limoncello and Prosecco are well chilled.

Makes 1 champagne flute
30ml (1fl oz) limoncello (see page 166 for homemade)
30ml (1fl oz) lemon granita
100ml (3½fl oz) Prosecco

Pour the limoncello into a champagne flute (or another glass you prefer), add the lemon granita and top with the Prosecco. Serve immediately. *Salute!*

COCKTAIL AL LIMONE

Lemon cocktail

This Campari and lemon cocktail came from the bar at Sal De Riso in Minori. They make lots of different lemon-inspired cocktails, but this is my favourite one. The lemon and sage and Italicus liqueurs can be obtained from good Italian delis or online. Use a cocktail shaker if you have one; if not, just use a cup with a secure lid to do your shaking. If you don't like the idea of raw egg white, then just omit it, but I like the foamy texture it adds to the cocktail.

Makes 2 cocktails
60ml (2fl oz) gin
50ml (1¾fl oz) lemon and sage liqueur
30ml (1fl oz) freshly squeezed lemon juice
20ml (½fl oz) Campari
10ml (2 tsp) Italicus Bergamot liqueur
ice cubes
1 egg white
2 lemon slices, to garnish

Place all the ingredients except for the egg white into a cocktail shaker and give it a good hard shake for about 30 seconds. Remove the ice cubes, add the egg white, shake again for 30 seconds and divide between two glasses. Garnish with the lemon slices and serve immediately. *Salute!*

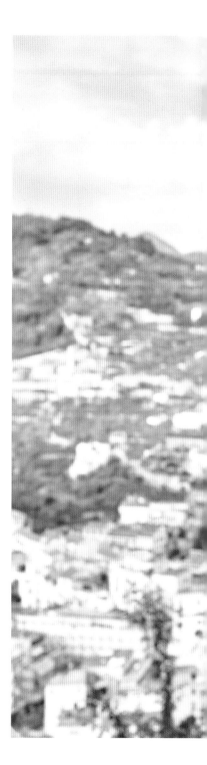

SUCCO DI LIMONE

Lemon Concentrate

This homemade concentrate is so handy to have for a refreshing drink at any time. You know what's in it and, as it's pure concentrate, you only need a small amount. So when you need refreshing, pour a little into a glass and top up with plain or sparkling water. For anyone with a cold or sore throat, dilute with hot water for a warm soothing drink. You can also make this with oranges, clementines and even grapefruits.

Makes approx. 500ml (18fl oz)
juice of 6 large lemons (you need 360ml/12¼fl oz juice),
    passed through a fine sieve
440g (15½oz) sugar
100ml (3½fl oz) water

Put all the ingredients in a saucepan along with 6 lemon halves and bring to the boil. Allow to boil for 10 minutes, stirring from time to time. Remove from the heat, place the lemon halves in a sieve or ricer and squeeze any juice back into the pan with the rest of the liquid. Discard the lemon halves. Pour the lemon concentrate into sterilized glass bottle/s, leave to cool, then seal tightly.

Store in the fridge. Once opened it will last for several weeks.

ESPRESSO CON BUCCIA DI LIMONE

Lemon Espresso

My day always starts with an espresso, to which I like to add a small piece of lemon rind. It's a habit I picked up from home in Italy; the lemon adds a refreshing citrus tang to the thick espresso coffee.

Serves 1
Make your espresso in the usual way in your machine. When ready, pour into a cup, add a small slice of lemon rind, making sure you have no white pith. Stir in sugar to taste and *buongiorno!*

MARMELLATA DI LIMONI

Lemon jam

Lemon jam is very popular in Italy and especially along the Amalfi Coast where lemons are plentiful. This really simple recipe, using just two ingredients, will make you want to make your own lemon jam all the time! It's perfect to spread on your morning toast but you could use it to sandwich sponge cakes or add to desserts. Leaving the lemon slices to soak in water will remove any bitter taste. This keeps well: double or treble the quantities if you wish to make more than a jar.

Makes 1 x 340g (11¾oz) jar
500g (1lb 2oz) unwaxed lemons
300g (10½oz) sugar

Sterilize your jar and lid by washing in hot soapy water, rinse then invert onto a baking tray and drying in a preheated oven at 160°C fan/180°C/gas mark 4 for 15 minutes.

Wash the lemons well under cold running water. Trim both ends of each one and thinly slice, removing any pips. Place the slices in a bowl and cover with plenty of cold water. Cover the bowl and leave for at least 12 hours, changing the water halfway through.

Drain off the water, put the lemon slices in a pan and mix well with the sugar. Place over the heat, bring to the boil and simmer rapidly for 30 minutes. You may want to check it has reached setting point by spooning a little on a cold saucer. If the jam wrinkles when you tilt the saucer, it is ready.

Remove from the heat and use a hand blender to blend gently so you get a nice combination of smooth jam with bits of peel. Of course, if you prefer it completely smooth, then blend away.

Pour into the sterilized jar and seal with a lid.

SAUCES & DRESSINGS

CONDIMENTO ALL'OLIO E LIMONE

Simple salad dressing

A perfect dressing for salads or try it poured over steamed vegetables and fish.

Makes approx. 90ml (3fl oz)
4 tbsp extra virgin olive oil
2 tbsp lemon juice
sea salt

Place all the ingredients into a small bowl and whisk for a couple of minutes until it goes creamy. Alternatively, put everything in a small bottle or jar, screw on the lid, and give it a good shake before serving.

MAIONESE AL LIMONE

Lemon mayo

I always find delicious, silky homemade mayonnaise much lighter than the shop-bought variety. Ensure you buy the best and freshest eggs you can and always use a light olive oil or sunflower oil. As much as I love extra virgin olive oil, it is just too overpowering for a mayonnaise. When you are adding the oil and lemon juice, make sure you add them very gradually: drop by drop is best to ensure you don't split the mayo (you may find you need a little more or less of the quantity of oil specified). For speed, use an electric whisk. Delicious served with simple steamed fish or whatever else you like to serve mayonnaise with. It will keep in the fridge, covered, for about 5 days as long as the eggs you use are fresh.

Serves 2
4 organic free-range egg yolks
pinch of sea salt
85ml (2¾fl oz) light olive or sunflower oil
20ml (½fl oz) lemon juice

Whisk the egg yolks with the salt until well combined. Gradually add the olive oil, drop by drop, while you continue to whisk until the mixture begins to thicken. At this point, gradually whisk in the lemon juice. Serve immediately or cover and place in the fridge until required.

BESCIAMELLA AL LIMONE

Lemon bechamel sauce

This lemon-infused white sauce combines perfectly with baked pasta dishes that include white fish or veggies, such as courgettes, spinach, Swiss chard or artichokes. Use this to make the Lasagne (see page 57).

Serves 4
40g (1½oz) butter
40g (1½oz) plain flour
500ml (18fl oz) milk
zest of 1 unwaxed lemon and juice of ½ lemon
sea salt, freshly ground black pepper
    and a pinch of grated nutmeg

Melt the butter in a saucepan over a medium heat, remove from the heat and whisk in the flour, then gradually add the milk, whisking all the time to avoid lumps. Return to the heat and continue to whisk until the sauce begins to thicken. Remove from the heat, stir in the lemon zest and juice and season with salt, pepper and nutmeg. Use immediately or cover and store in the fridge until required.

SALSINA ALLA SICILIANA

Sicilian dressing

This Sicilian-inspired dressing can be used warm or cold, poured over steamed fish, on salads or delicious to dip bread into. If you can find fresh oregano, do use it.

Serves 4
4 tbsp extra virgin olive oil
juice of 1 lemon
½ tsp dried oregano
5 fresh oregano leaves, finely chopped (optional)
½ garlic clove, very finely chopped
pinch of dried red chilli
pinch of sea salt

Combine all the ingredients in a small pan over a medium heat, whisking from time to time, for about 5–7 minutes until it begins to thicken slightly. Remove from the heat and use immediately or cover and store in the fridge for up to a month.

GREMOLADA

This is traditionally a topping for the classic Milanese dish ossobuco (braised veal shanks). But you could also use it to sprinkle on other stews, fish, pasta or any other savoury dish for a burst of freshness. If you like, you could add a couple of anchovies or, for an extra citrussy taste, some orange zest.

Serves 4
2 garlic cloves, finely chopped
zest of 1 unwaxed lemon
handful of fresh flat-leaf parsley, finely chopped

Combine all the ingredients and use accordingly.

SALSA VERDE AL LIMONE

Lemon salsa verde

Salsa verde is a classic Italian sauce which goes well with meat and fish dishes. I also love it on crostini or simply for dipping in some good bread. It is often made with vinegar, but is equally delicious with lemon juice – and for those who find the taste of vinegar too strong, this is ideal.

Serves 4
30g (1oz) crustless stale country bread,
    soaked in a little water
a large handful of flat-leaf parsley
½ garlic clove
1 hard-boiled egg
10g (¼oz) salted capers, rinsed
2 anchovy fillets, rinsed if salted
zest and juice of ½ unwaxed lemon
90ml (6 tbsp) olive oil

Take the bread and use your hands to squeeze out the excess water, then finely chop. Finely chop the parsley, garlic, egg, capers, anchovies and the lemon zest. Combine with the lemon juice and olive oil.

Alternatively, if you are in a hurry or prefer the consistency smoother, whizz all the ingredients in a blender.

186   Limoni

SALSA DI BURRO, LIMONE E MENTA

Butter, lemon and mint sauce

This sauce is ideal for stirring through spaghetti for a quick meal and for more elaborate filled pasta dishes, such as Mezzelune with lemon and ricotta (see page 52).

Serves 4
100g (3½oz) butter
20 mint leaves
4 tsp lemon juice
40g (1¼oz) Parmesan cheese, grated

Put the butter and mint in a frying pan over a medium heat, allow the butter to melt, then add the lemon juice and cook until the butter begins to bubble. Stir in the grated Parmesan. Add cooked pasta, loosen with a little of the cooking water and mix well.

SALSINA DI ACCIUGHE CAPPERI E LIMONE

Caper, anchovy and lemon dressing

If you love anchovies, this is the dressing for you! Perfect to pour over steamed white fish or on salads.

Serves 4
4 anchovy fillets
2 tsp capers
5 tbsp extra virgin olive oil
juice of ½ lemon
sea salt and freshly ground black pepper

Very finely chop the anchovies until they resemble a paste. Very finely chop the capers. Set aside.

Whisk the extra virgin olive oil and lemon juice together until it begins to thicken slightly. Stir in the anchovy paste, capers and a little salt and pepper to taste, but be careful how much salt you add as anchovies and capers are quite salty.

Pour into a container and use as required. Before using, give it a quick whisk. Store in the fridge for up to a month.

CREMA PASTICCIERA AL LIMONE

Lemon custard

Nothing beats homemade custard and, once you know how easy it is to make, you will never go back to buying the ready-made version. This delicious lemon custard can be enjoyed as it is, poured over sponge, used in trifles, as a sweet tart filling (see the Lemon Tart on page 144) or however else you enjoy custard.

Serves 4–6
6 egg yolks
130g (4¾oz) caster sugar
50g (1¾oz) plain flour
500ml (18fl oz) hot (not boiling) milk
pared rind of ½ unwaxed lemon (no white pith)
8 tsp lemon juice

In a saucepan, whisk together the egg yolks and sugar for about 5 minutes until the sugar has dissolved and the mixture is smooth and creamy. Add the flour and continue to whisk until well amalgamated. Whisk in the hot milk and lemon rind, then place the pan over a low heat, stirring all the time with the whisk or a wooden spoon, until it thickens. Remove from the heat and stir in the lemon juice.

Serve hot or cold or cover and store in the fridge until required (it will last up to 3 days). Remember to discard the lemon rind before serving.

INDEX

ACKNOWLEDGEMENTS

Liz Przybylski for writing, testing recipes and organising me!

Adriana Contaldo for testing recipes and cooking at the shoots.

David Loftus for wonderful photos and lovely days spent in Minori.

Jodene Jordan for beautiful food styling and props.

Penny Forster-Brown for your help at the shoots.

Carmine and Jacopo Porporra for their invaluable help with organising the shoot in Minori.

Alessandro and Franco Gambardella and their amazing father, Gabriele, who is a master pastry chef and still bakes at his Pasticceria Gambardella in Minori. Also thanks to all his staff at the pastry shop for their help and delicious pastries.

Erminia Carrano for her delicious rabbit dish and to her husband Andrea.

Giuliano and Giuseppe Ruocco for beautiful plates.

Filippo Milo and Fabio for allowing us to shoot at their lovely Orto Paradiso.

Michele Apuzzo the greengrocer and Carlo De Riso of Costagrumi for wonderful lemons.

Giovanni and Antonio Di Bianco and family and all the staff at Giardiniello Restaurant. A special thanks to the chef for creating the beautiful fish dish.

Salvatore de Riso and staff at Sal de Riso for wonderful cakes and cocktails.

Valentino Esposito of Gusto della Costa and his lovely family for their invaluable help and delicious limoncello!

Jamie Oliver for using lemons in his cooking all the time!

Laura Russell, Helen Lewis, Sophie Allen and Komal Patel at Pavilion.